WHAT'S IN A NAME: Famous Brand Names

Do you think you'd ever go up to a soda fountain and order *Erythroxylon coca* juice? Sounds better as Coke, doesn't it? Or would you care for a piece of *polyvinyl acetate*? Not much pizzazz in *that* bubble gum! A light-hearted look at the origins and development of some masterpieces of the art and science of names, and their importance in products that have become an integral part of the American—and world—scene.

WHAT'S IN A NAME
Famous Brand Names

By

Oren Arnold

 Julian Messner   New York

Library of Congress Cataloging in Publication Data

Arnold, Oren.
    What's in a name.

    Includes index.
    SUMMARY: Discusses the origin and development of well-
known products and the importance of their brand names.
    1.   Business names—United States—Juvenile literature.
2.   Business names—Juvenile literature.   3.   Trade-
marks—United States—Juvenile literature.   4.   Trade-
marks—Juvenile literature.   [1.   Trademarks]   I.   Title.
HF5827.A733   658.8'27'0973   79-15555
ISBN 0-671-32932-4

Dedicated with love
to Wendy Lee and Sharon Gail

C /

ACKNOWLEDGMENTS

Many talented people helped in the research for this book and in checking the manuscript. The author is grateful to each of them. Very special thanks go to Mr. Barry R. Detwiler, at the University of Southern California; also to a distinguished former teacher of young teenagers who is an author of books on teaching techniques, Adele R. Arnold, and to her friend who has long worked with young people in high school and junior college levels, Martha Maxwell; also to Mr. Robert F. Decker, who has had extensive experience in merchandising and trade-name promotion on three continents, and to his talented wife Jeanne.

CONTENTS

INTRODUCTION

From the moment you got out of bed this morning, your life began to be influenced by famous brand names.

The influence will continue until you crawl back between the covers tonight. Even then the sheets, the blankets, the pillows will have special trademark-registered names owned by the companies that manufactured them. How did they get those names?

How does *any* product get its special name? Why is it called *Coca Cola*, or *Scotch Tape*, or *Jell-O*, or *Life Savers*, or *Birds Eye*, or *Kodak*? There are hundreds of thousands of them, and the importance of those names is seldom recognized.

They are important not only to their owners, the business people who create and promote them; they influence the lives of almost every citizen in America and Canada and around the world. They thrust themselves at us from every billboard, newspaper, magazine, television screen and radio commercial. They pop out in beautiful print that comes in the mail. They are written in white across our blue skies by airplanes. Most of all, they are encountered moment by moment in our homes, tacked or printed on our furniture, sewn into our clothing, welded onto our automobiles and other machinery, and printed on the endless bags and boxes that we use—especially those carried into our kitchens.

Even so, we take them for granted; we give them scarcely a passing thought.

The stories behind these names are fascinating—not just the choosing of the names themselves, but the development of the products they represent. Great pride enters those endeavors; the whole lives of brilliant, dedicated men and women are involved. Imagination, courage, romance, adventure, frustration, persistence, creativity, failure, triumph—even humor—are revealed in these true stories.

Studying trade names is one way to understand and appreciate big business around the world today. It is a fun thing to do: education with a sugar coating.

Chapter 1

The Marvelous Story of Coca Cola

Of all the things that people eat, chew, drink, wear, ride in, or otherwise use, none is as famous as Coca Cola.

Worldwide demand for Coca Cola is almost unbelievable. Coke is an accepted part of living, taken for granted almost like water itself. For many years Coke was sold only in soda fountains or in bottles holding just six ounces. The peak sales even then passed 50,000,000 bottles every day, not to mention the uncounted millions of glasses served over the counter.

In mid-century, Coke became prominent in dispensing machines seen everywhere. Total sales have recently been increased again by use of bottles and cans in several new sizes. Today the major retail outlet for Coca Cola is not the soda fountain but the grocery store. Millions pick up cartons and large bottles for their home refrigerators.

Naturally, the question arises—*why?*

Why has such fame and popularity come to this little soft drink, which after all is not really important to our health, happiness or general welfare?

The answer is clear. Coke is mildly stimulating, somewhat like coffee, and it has a pleasant taste. But the

13

main reason for its popularity is the most extensive advertising campaign ever known.

In this century, billions of dollars have been spent for space in magazines and newspapers and on signboards, for time on radio and television, telling us about Coca Cola. Actually, very little is told, ever. But in the world of publicity and advertising, repetition builds reputation. We see it and see it and hear it and hear it almost every hour day in and day out, until the name becomes etched on our brains before we even enter kindergarten. By the time we are age ten or twelve, Coca Cola or its nickname Coke is a part of our household language, much as are milk and bread.

How did Coca Cola get its name in the first place?

The answer requires a bit of background knowledge. Coke is a soda water, which is the general name that applies to all bubbly, fizzy soft drinks. Yet none of those has any soda in it. When you put a little ordinary kitchen soda (bicarbonate of soda, or sodium bicarbonate) into a glass of water, bubbles arise so that the water fizzes or seems charged with gas, but it does *not* taste good. However, another chemical put into the water gives the same bubbly effect, and many people think this mixture does taste good. This chemical is the basis of all soda waters.

They began about two centuries ago when a renowned scientist, Priestly, bubbled some carbonic acid gas through plain water. He tasted the resulting mixture and liked it. Then he went into his garden, picked ripe blackberries, squeezed their juice into the glass of charged water and drank again. Now the mixture was really delicious—and "soda water" had been born. Soon Mr. Priestly began making that carbonic acid-water-blackberry juice in bucketsful and peddling it in small bottles. He named his fancy new drink *Phosphate ferrozodone*. Can you imagine ordering a refreshing, cooling bottle of soda by that name today?

From the start, many new mixtures were evolved and offered under names. All of them came in time to be called soda water and, later, soda pop. The word "pop" came from the fact that ordinary cork stoppers, used at first, were replaced by a hard wire loop attached to a rubber disc in the neck of each bottle. This loop stuck out about half an inch when the bottle was sealed. To get at the soda, you had to hit the wire loop firmly with the palm of your hand. A rather loud *pop* resulted. Instantly the drink squirted and fizzed out all over your hands and likely onto your friends nearby—great fun, but wasteful. Pop top popping was one of the high moments at any youth party prior to 1912 or so. The metal clamp top, the screw-on cap, and the pull-tab on cans, all are relatively new.

Among those soda waters, Coca Cola both as a drink and a name is a Johnny-come-lately. Not until after the American Civil War did it appear, and not until after World War I did it begin to soar toward such great popularity as it enjoys today.

John Pemberton Invented It.

When the Civil War ended, thousands of men were hard put to earn a living, especially in the defeated South where Reconstruction was chaotic. Money was scarce and jobs were scarcer, so the discharged Confederate veterans tried anything they could dream up that might be profitable. One of them, John S. Pemberton, decided to become a pharmacist because there was a need for a drugstore in the burned-out town of Atlanta. Mostly on credit, he opened a small drugstore.

Pemberton was not a very good merchant because he became more interested in chemistry than selling. Most of his time was spent back in his private room mixing chemicals, trying to create new healing salves and medicines.

But John also did a lot of experimenting with soft drinks. ("Soft" means nonalcoholic.) In that era, the usual soft drink was called sarsaparilla, named that for its flavor base, the sarsaparilla vine growing in Brazil, Central America and Mexico. It was correctly pronounced *sar-sah-pah-REE-yah*, but youths of that time usually called it "sappy-riller." Its taste was pleasant but very mild. John Pemberton hoped to create a drink with more clout, more distinctive flavor appeal. He kept mixing various chemicals with that charged water, then adding sugar and tasting the results.

Finally he had a formula that to him tasted exceptionally good. It was a black-brown liquid, somewhat like strong tea in appearance. Its appearance was against it, he feared, because people of that era tended to favor drinks that were rich pink. Pink lemonade was a standard refreshment at circuses, carnivals, church suppers and home parties. He could find no way to make his tasty new drink pink or clear. But after swigging down a glass of it, John would feel a lift of energy for an hour or two afterward.

This was much like the effect of coffee or strong tea.

Would people take to his stimulating drink in spite of its ugly color? He wondered. And without knowing it, he was at the crux of one of the greatest business ventures in human history. He might simply have become discouraged or disgusted, thrown his formula away and forgotten it.

In point of fact, John really was *not* much interested in his new drink. It was just something he had casually mixed up in the back room of his pharmacy, and it seemed to hold little promise. So he set the formula aside for awhile. After all, a pharmacist had to make a living, and his business wasn't doing well. This was in May of 1886. His world was still struggling to get over the tragic effects of the war, and in his home town of Atlanta almost everybody still faced hard times.

One day he did find time to restudy his black-brown drink. He felt it needed more testing on consumers, men and women, boys and girls. So he went into the yard behind his red brick house, which had been built before the war and somehow survived, and built a fire under an old iron pot that had been used for boiling clothes.

He put liquids that matched the formula for his drink into the pot to be blended by a little boiling. The pot held a quantity enough for him to share with his friends. All this was simply a kind of hobby with John, a sideline to his work. At the moment, he wasn't concerned with a name for the drink.

But John Pemberton had a friend, also a former Confederate soldier, who was now the bookkeeper in the pharmacy. His name was Frank M. Robinson. Being more bookish-minded than chemical-minded, he told John that all drinks should have names, just as all medicines had names. The druggist agreed, though he was not much interested. Frank Robinson put his mind to it.

He asked his friend John what the main chemicals in his drink were. One of them, said John, was obtained from the leaf of a shrub grown mostly in Bolivia. It was known by the botanical name of *Erythroxylon coca*. (*Coca* is not the same *cocoa* or *cacao* from which chocolate is made. Chocolate comes from the seed or bean of another plant.)

Frank Robinson studied that strange botanical name. He could see no way to use both words, but the single word *coca* had possibilities. It was short, easy to say, easy to remember. He asked John what else was in his new drink.

The other main ingredient, said John, was an extract from the nut of either of two kinds of *kola* trees growing in the tropics. Those nuts held some caffeine, a stimulant to the heart and central nervous system, the same potent drug found in coffee.

So now Frank had two words—*coca* and *kola*. He mulled them over in his mind. They were short and alliterative, easy to say, easy to remember. He began to doodle them with pencil on paper, and changed the *k* to a *c*. He wrote *coca cola*, and for a time went around muttering the words or saying them aloud—"coca cola, coca cola, coca cola." Yes, he decided, it seemed like a distinctive and pleasing name for a drink. At least it was better than "phosphate ferrozodone." It could catch on in public fancy, especially if advertised a little.

He went a step further and very carefully wrote the name in a beautiful flourishing script, with the top of the *C* in Cola extending in a graceful curve through the loop of the *l*. It was pleasing to the eye.

With little change, that "Coca Cola" design or logo is the one you see today.

As a brand name, it is seen, accepted, and taken for granted as a routine part of life around the world. The total number of times it has appeared must be far into the billions. For no other name or product in history has ever had so much money spent on it. You well know how often it appears; seemingly there is no escape from it.

Usually a few additional words accompany that written trade name. For years billboards and other advertisements said simply—"Coca Cola . . . Quenches Thirst." It still does quench thirst, although plain water does also.

Since then, new slogans have been used. They are devised, brainstormed, and tested by highly paid experts. They are carefully studied for "consumer impact and motivation" before millions of dollars are spent on printing and distribution. Recent new slogans say of Coca Cola that "It's The Real Thing," which is vague, but an effective slap at competitive cola drinks, a bid to increase sales.

John Started
With 25 Gallons.

Back there in 1886, John Pemberton boiled up twenty-five gallons in his iron wash pot. He had to ask himself what he could possibly do with it. Not even his friends could drink that much. Sell it?

Because he was a druggist, his thinking leaned toward other drugstores, most of which were already beginning to install soda fountains as a sideline to their main business. Nobody quite knows why drugstores went in for

soft-drink or fountain refreshments. Why not the grocery
stores or clothing stores? But somehow druggists sensed
that offering sarsaparilla and other drinks would make
their stores popular places to go, hangouts for boys and
girls, pleasant places for weary adults to drop in and rest.

John went to one of his colleagues and talked him into
offering Coca Cola for sale. People who dared test it liked
it. Because of its stimulating quality, it had repeat appeal. Atlanta did not have many soda fountains, but
John talked them all into offering Coca Cola. By the end
of the year, his entire twenty-five gallons of basic Coca
Cola syrup had been sold.

In each drugstore he had to teach the "mixers"—the
forerunner of "soda jerkers"—to put barely half an inch
of the thick, dark syrup in the bottom of six-ounce glasses,
then stir in the charged soda water. A little ice could be
added if desired. Some people thought the warm drink
was better, just as some people today prefer their beer
warm rather than chilled. Soon, almost everybody
wanted crushed ice, which begat another industry, sup-
plying clean crushed ice to soda-dispensing stores.

By the end of 1886, John Pemberton had already
launched the Coca Cola advertising program; to promote
the drink he had spent $46. Friends thought he was
tetched for spending money so foolishly.

Such, then, was the launching. With no great fanfare,
fame or acclaim, Coca Cola was added to the list of popular American drinks and brand names. It was talked
about both pro and con. Many people opposed it because
of its chemical composition.

Onto the American scene in the first decades of the
twentieth century came not only a popular new drink but

a new piece of slang. The Coca Cola slogan "Delicious and Refreshing" was used as a sophisticated label for whatever people liked. The new and personable school teacher was "delicious and refreshing." The New Girl in Town was also, if she happened to be pretty and vivacious. Coconut cake or cranberry pie was "delicious and refreshing." The new song that launched ragtime music, *Alexander's Ragtime Band*, was "refreshing and delicious." Of course the Coca Cola people were delighted; reputation-by-association was to their advantage. Let others worry about Coca Cola's bad qualities, Coca Cola was "the bee's knees, the cat's meow."

John Pemberton would have been astounded and no doubt pleased. Regrettably, he had died only two years after that first backyard boiling of the twenty-five gallons, quite unaware that he had launched not only a drink but a trade name that was to become a facet of everyday life.

Asa G. Chandler
Bought All the Rights.

Among John's friends was another young Atlanta pharmacist, Asa G. Chandler. Asa had tasted Coca Cola and liked it. He saw a chance to peddle it not only to soda fountains in Atlanta but in other cities as well. So he gave up his job, paid $2,300 for complete ownership of Coca Cola as a chemical formula and as a trademarked name. Today, the cost would have to be nearer $23 billion.

Asa set out at once to expand sales, devoting full time to promotion and selling. In 1892 he organized a corporation called The Coca Cola Company. Three years later he was selling his drink in every one of the American states.

Then in Chattanooga, Tennessee, a lawyer named Benjamin F. Thomas and a friend, Joseph B. Whitehead, decided that if Coca Cola was popular as a fountain drink, it might also be sold profitably in bottles. Thousands of people could not always be near a soda fountain when they felt thirsty. They went to Atlanta and talked with Asa Chandler.

Mr. Chandler had his doubts. The bottles would cost a lot of money. They would easily break. They would be heavy and require costly handling—loading the wagons with care, hauling them around, packing everything against breakage, shipping on trains, reclaiming and washing them. How could it pay off?

But the two men from Chattanooga were optimistic, so Mr. Chandler agreed to let them try bottling. No, they could *not* manufacture the basic Coca Cola syrup; Mr. Chandler would legally retain that right, but he would sell them all they wanted. No doubt he felt quite shrewd. The two friends returned to Chattanooga, raised $5,000 and started bottling.

**Bottling
By Hand.**

At first, all bottling had to be done by hand. Mix the syrup in a vat with charged water, pour it carefully through a funnel into glass bottles held between the knees, hammer in corks very tight, pack the bottles in cottonseed hulls or other soft material in boxes, put the boxes on horse-drawn wagons, and carry the drink around to sell to people. It was hard, tedious work, and usually there was no way to ice the bottles. Yet the faith of the two friends paid off; people did take to the bottled drink, iced or not. So the time, money and effort spent began to reap a profit.

Mr. Chandler wasn't too interested in all that. He was doing very well selling his drink to soda fountains. Therefore, he sold the legal right to bottle and sell Coca Cola in all the states for less than $100. Financially, it was one of the biggest mistakes in the history of American business.

**Beyond Anybody's
Fondest Dreams.**

From that point, the true story of Coca Cola becomes one of the biggest in big business anywhere. Sales zoomed beyond expectations. From hundreds of bottles sold each week, the quantity leaped to thousands, then hundreds of thousands a day. For a while during World War I, no Coca Cola was available in many towns, because the two main ingredients could not then be imported easily. Those towns spoke of it as a national tragedy and hated Germany all the more for depriving them.

Today, the franchise just for the privilege of bottling Coca Cola—the permit alone, not the machinery or the materials—in any one city usually costs several million dollars.

Variations often enter into names. Nicknames tend to take over. Jonathan becomes Johnny or John. Maria Louisa becomes Marylou or even Maylu. That happened to Coca Cola. Somehow, spontaneously, around 1920, Coca Cola became Coke.

Coca Cola people were at first appalled and worried. The Coca Cola owners felt that the nickname tended to belittle their drink, and they began to plead with the public to use the full, correct name, advertising also to "Accept No Substitutes." The latter was an obvious warfare against other, similar drinks.

But Americans ignored the plea and went right on asking for Cokes. The rival bottlers also began hearing their cola drinks called "Coke." The Coca Cola Company became alarmed; hundreds of millions of dollars were at stake. They went to court to stop other cola drinks from being called Coke.

The business details are long and involved. But the high courts ruled the Coca Cola Company could have sole ownership not only of its real name but of its nickname as well. That ruling was worth millions, perhaps billions, of dollars to the company. Today both names are duly registered with the federal government in Washington, and nobody else may use either name for selling a drink.

Competition.

However, the word *cola* was left open for use by anybody. Thus today we have such Coke rivals as Pepsi Cola, RC Cola and others. Even the local grocery chain often bottles a drink made primarily from coca leaves and the kola bean and gives it a local name—Ralph's Cola, or Smith's Cola, etc.

Pepsi and RC and some other brands are making fortunes, too, competing aggressively with Coke. The Coke people claim to have a secret formula. As recently as

1977 the government of India was trying to break down the exact formula, threatening to boycott unless it was revealed.

India need not have worried because any good chemist can make an exact qualitative-quantitative analysis of Coke. This is commonly done by bright students in high school chemistry classes. Even so, the Coke hierarchy will rarely admit that its formula has been broken down.

Coca Cola has one other registered item owned exclusively by the company—the small, fluted, curved bottle. Art experts have called it the most perfectly designed merchandising package in the world.

It seems unlikely that either Coca Cola or Pepsi Cola will suffer any severe financial setbacks in the foreseeable future. In the late 1970s, the market for each product suddenly expanded astronomically.

Pepsi Cola made a firm deal with the Soviet Union, whereby Pepsi could be sold throughout Russia —exclusive of any other American cola drink.

The Coca Cola executives were naturally disturbed by Pepsi's coup. The vast Russian outlet could put Pepsi in first place in world sales. Prestige of the trade names —Coca Cola and Coke—was endangered.

The Coke executives moved rapidly, but quietly, studying world affairs, especially American diplomacy, looking for a market. Relations between the USA and Asian nations were improving. President Nixon had made a notable trip, reopening relations with the Peoples Republic of China. President Carter's administration gave full recognition to the Republic of China in 1978. And so, the powerful Coca Cola Company countered Pepsi's coup by making an even bigger deal with Peking.

The terms stated that, for the first time in history, bottled Coke could be exported to China. Soon the Coke syrup itself would be sent in and bottled by Chinese labor there. It was an exclusive contract, for Coca Cola alone, and opened up the potential for a market of more than a billion people.

The United States has only some 220 million people. Even Russia has nowhere near as many people as China. (Exact counts are unknown.) The Chinese are said to be fascinated with Coke already. This is partly because they see it as a new and inexpensive luxury, in a realm where even small luxuries for the masses are in short supply.

Can you envision that long border between Russia and China, with gigantic signboards on the north side shouting, "Pepsi Cola hits the spot," and those on the south side shouting back, "Coca Cola—It's the real thing"? Anyway, it's a fun war.

Chapter 2

Great Gums

Another popular youthful pleasure is the chewing of bubble gum. There can be no exact count, but it is estimated that for each bottle of Coke drunk, at least one tidbit of bubble gum is popped into the mouth.

Since about 1975 even adults have taken to bubble gum with astounding eagerness. Psychologists suggest that this unpredicted, unprecedented popularity is due simply to the pure fun of chewing and blowing out a pink-balloon bubble. It is a harmless, inexpensive, though somewhat indelicate pleasure.

In 1970 bubble gum sales accounted for only 10 percent of American chewing gum sales. By late 1978, bubble gum had 33 percent of the total gum market and was expected to have 50 percent of it by 1980. In 1977, more than 1 million pounds of bubble gum were sold in the United States. That is nearly one-half pound for every man, woman and child.

The fad suddenly swept the nation, as never before, in 1977-78. It is thought to have been triggered by professional baseball. First, one popular pitcher was repeatedly shown on television at the pitcher's mound, leaning over to catch his pitching signal, calmly blowing a big pink balloon out of his mouth. The idea caught on. By late summer of 1978, an estimated 80 percent of all pro and amateur baseball players were chewing and ballooning bubble gum.

The famed Los Angeles Dodgers and New York Mets held a public bubble-blowing contest among their players televised before their game in New York City's Shea Stadium. Rick Rhoden of the Dodgers was photographed close-up blowing out a bubble measuring 14 inches across—but lost the contest to the Mets' Bobby Valentine whose bubble measured 15 inches. Photos of the contest turned up on front pages of newspaper sports sections across the continent and abroad. Never mind the home runs, or the final scores of the game—the BIG show that day was bubble blowing.

The next day, bubble gum supplies in thousands of stores were sold out before noon, and owners hurriedly ordered more.

It's Chicle— Isn't It?

If you ask any alert gum addict, you will probably be told that he or she is chewing chicle, the dried sap of a jungle tree. If he is really knowledgeable, he may add that the tree is called *sapodilla* (sah-po-DEE-yah) and that the sap is obtained only by the effort of workmen braving the dangers of thick, tropical forests.

It's not so.

No wilderness is involved; bubble gum is not chicle but plastic.

The scientific name for it is *polyvinyl acetate*. Synthetic or imitation chicle is produced by a manufacturer of explosives, the Hercules Powder Company. Chewing gum thus has acquired a new family tree.

That fact takes some of the glamour away. Therefore, manufacturers try not to mention it.

In polite society, chewing any kind of gum is considered inelegant. Many persons frown on it. They are unhappy in the presence of brash people who chew gum rapidly and noisily. They also take a dim view of that pink bubble which balloons out and bursts.

Nevertheless, in one given year consumers paid a whopping $622,000,000 for chewing gum—more than twice the amount spent a decade earlier. A further increase of about 15 percent a year was under way, as this book was being written.

Thus it could be said that the opinion of nonchewers does not really disturb gumchewers; gum is a trivial pleasure, and others do not have to look. The gum chewer simply smiles at their sensitivity and reaches for one of his or her favorite brandname gums.

As with Coca Cola and Coke, almost everyone over age six is familiar with "Wrigley's Spearmint Chewing Gum" or "Wrigley's Doublemint Chewing Gum." Other brands are almost as well known, for instance; "Beechnut," "Chiclets," "Beeman's," "Dentyne," and "Dubble Bubble."

Millions of dollars have been spent advertising chewing gums, especially Wrigley's. Some people wonder how so trivial a product as a little blob of gum can add up to big business.

Let's answer it this way. The Wrigley family bought an

entire, famous and very beautiful island located 30 miles
off the coast of California and built a lovely resort town
there—all on the profits from chewing gum. Later they
bought a small mountain in the most fashionable and
costly part of modern Phoenix, Arizona, and built a man-
sion on top resembling a castle in Europe. They also own
a big league baseball team, fine houses in Chicago and
elsewhere.

Even if the company profit is only a fraction of a cent
per chew, the total still mounts rapidly. Extensive advertising has made us conscious of gum names; Wrigley's is
virtually a part of the language, just like Coke. Almost
half the gum we chew is made by Wrigley.

**A Mexican General
Started It.**

The story behind chewing gum begins, surprisingly, with
a man once hated by thousands of Americans, especially
Texans. His name was General Antonio Lopez de Santa
Anna.

About 140 years ago he commanded an army for the
Republic of Mexico. In that era Texas was a part of
Mexico. However, the Texans declared Texas independ-
ent, a separate nation. Mexico sent General Santa Anna
and a strong army to punish the Texans.

Santa Anna had initial success. He massacred a few
hundred Texans in the Alamo, a mission fortress at San
Antonio. A short time later he and his army were cor-
nered and defeated by an army under General Sam
Houston at San Jacinto, a field about 24 miles out of the
present metropolis of Houston.

General Santa Anna was brought in alive. Most people wanted to stand him before a firing squad and execute him. But General Sam Houston said that Santa Anna must live, as a guarantee of peace with Mexico. So they sent him and his servants to a safer area in faraway New York.

Among the possessions that Santa Anna took eastward with him was a box containing a large quantity of chicle from the sapodilla trees in Mexico—in other words, chewing gum. Who would have thought that a renowned army general was a gum chewer? But Santa Anna was part Aztec Indian, and the Aztecs had long chewed chicle for pleasure, so he had acquired the habit.

Easterners showed interest in the captured general. Some yearned to kill him, others tried to lionize him. An inventor named Thomas Adams, who lived in Jersey City, near New York, managed to get an introduction to him, and soon Santa Anna showed him his chicle and started talking business.

The general's idea was that his chewable, stretchable sap from a tree could be used as a substitute for rubber if it were properly refined. Would Mr. Adams be interested? He was, but extensive tests of the chicle ended in failure. Rubber is also a tree sap, but chicle did not have its strength. Disappointed, General Santa Anna glumly resumed chewing the soft, tasteless chicle to calm his nerves.

Among those who saw the general chewing was Adams' son Horatio. He started chewing chicle and enjoyed it. One day Horatio happened to see a little girl buy some ordinary paraffin in a drugstore and start chewing it.

Paraffin is a waxy clear or white substance, much like

candle wax, made from petroleum, the same under-
ground oil from which we get gasoline. It has little or no
taste, but was chewed in various forms for fun. Horatio
Adams tried it.

Quickly he realized that his chicle from Santa Anna
was a much better chew, more pliable, less apt to gum up
the teeth, and better tasting. He conferred with his father. Together they bought $50 worth of additional
chicle, mixed it with boiling water and kneaded it into
marble-sized balls. They took two hundred of these balls
to a druggist who agreed to try to sell them.

The balls sold quickly for one cent each—and the
chewing gum industry was on its way.

**"Snapping and
Stretching."**

Horatio next rented an old factory loft in Jersey City,
cleaned it out and began processing his gum there. He
soon realized that hand-rolling the chicle into balls took
too much time, so he devised a machine to run the gum
out in long, flat strips. The merchants could cut them
into penny lengths. He put the strips into boxes labeled
"Adams' New York Gum—Snapping and Stretching."

Merchants all over town began buying the boxes and
making a good profit. Then Horatio's brother, Thomas
Adams, Jr., took a supply westward and placed the gum
on sale in many cities. Everyone took to the gooey, tasteless chicle.

This minor business success inspired Horatio Adams to
do new research. He wanted a better product, something
with a real come-on, buy-again appeal. So, he decided to

give his gum a better taste. First, he put a little sap from the sassafras tree into the chicle. Nobody liked the taste. Next he put some licorice into the gum, and everybody liked it! Licorice was already a popular flavor for candy. Horatio called his licorice gum "Black Jack." It proved to be a good name which is still used.

Other people soon observed that the Adams brothers were making money with the sticky sap from tropical trees and hastened to try marketing it themselves. One was a druggist in Louisville, Kentucky, named John Colgan, who was successful in adding balsam extract to his chicle and naming the product "Tuolo-flavored Gum." Balsam has a pleasant odor associated with green forests, and the public was pleased.

Then, along came a bookkeeper named Nellie Horton who worked for Edward E. Beeman, a druggist and manufacturer of a compound called pepsin. In the year 1880 Miss Horton suggested that Beeman try mixing a little of pleasant-smelling pepsin with chewing gum and offering it for sale. Mr. Beeman did, and soon his "peppermint" gum was a runaway success.

Pepsin, however, is not the same as peppermint; they just happen to smell and taste somewhat alike. Pepsin is a chemical extract from the stomachs of cows, sheep and other animals, a digestive juice. Peppermint is the sap of the fragrant mint plant. So real peppermint, a long-time favorite, was soon added to gum instead of pepsin.

The Mint Gum-Hog
In Advertising!

Ed Beeman had some rather far-out ideas about advertising. He had the picture of a hog printed on the wrappers of his tasty new peppermint gum. People wondered what a hog had to do with chewing gum.

He had the answer, at least in his own mind: the picture would induce people to chew his gum in quantities, as a hog eats. If we today think much of our own modern advertising (on television and in print) is ridiculous or silly, there is some precedent in Mr. Beeman's hog. The picture on his gum became something of a national joke.

Even so, it did not seem to hinder the sale of his mint-flavored gum. Perhaps the hog really did its job, getting the gum talked about, advertised by word of mouth—which is the best advertising of all. In any event, the growing popularity of the gum attracted the attention of a banker in Cleveland, Ohio, George Worthy. He approached Mr. Beeman, suggesting an expanded business which he would finance. Beeman agreed. The first thing Worthy ordered was an end to the hog picture and the placing of Mr. Beeman's own portrait, beard and all, on the chewing gum wrapper. Within a year or two Mr. Beeman was nationally renowned because millions of people were fingering his portrait as they popped a piece of gum into their mouths. His picture appeared until about 1960, although he died in 1906. Beeman's gum is still one of the popular brands.

In the 1880s, when Beeman "perfected" chewing gum by introducing the mint flavor, people felt that the very peak of success had been reached. They were sure there wasn't anything else that anybody could do to it. People were enjoying gum for very little money. Tropical chicle, flavored with mint, sold for a penny a stick; a small luxury, with no room for improvement.

Not so! A popcorn salesman, Bill White, changed the picture. Bill himself nursed no great dreams of achievement; he merely thought about earning a living and being content. But Bill had a groceryman friend. One day the grocer opened what he had ordered as a barrel of nuts. To his dismay, inside were no nuts, but only a mass of hardened sap from the tropical trees called chicle. Wasn't that the stuff from which chewing gum was made?

"Popcorn Bill."

"Popcorn Bill" happened to be in the store that morning, and the disgusted grocer gave him the barrel of chicle to get it out of the way. Bill wasn't sure what to do with it, either. Grinning friends in town heard about the mistake and asked questions. "It is petrified bread," happy-natured Bill told them, "found in the ruins of ancient Pompeii, the city buried centuries ago by the volcano Vesuvius." But Bill had an inquiring mind. He had the chicle on his hands and time to experiment. He learned that with a little boiling water the chicle could be kneaded and put into any shape desired, and then chewed. So in his spare time, he tried an experiment, adding a bit of corn syrup to a batch of the gum.

He gave some to neighborhood children who liked its sweet taste. Candy was often too sweet, but with this gum you could enjoy a candylike interval of sugar taste, then have the gum left to chew and chew and chew. The standard gum of the day—Beeman's—had only mint flavor, no sweetener.

Bill put his sweetened gum on the market, and before

he realized it he was a millionaire. Because his chicle came from the tropical peninsula of Yucatan, he named his delicious chew "Yucatan Gum." He became nationally known for revolutionizing the industry. All other manufacturers had to start adding sugar in some form to their chicle. Bill White, who had no dream of glory at all, now was the flashily dressed and wealthy escort of famous actresses in New York City. He used the photo of one, Miss Anna Held, in his gum advertising. She chewed his gum in public, told newspaper reporters how delicious it was, and they published her opinion. In gratitude, Bill gave her a necklace of pearls that reputedly cost him $150,000—how much would that be today?

With his new fame and fortune, Bill also entered politics. He ran for Congress and was elected. Then he went to England and managed to get an audience with the reigning monarch, King Edward VII. There he startled the Royal Court by presenting His Majesty with a box of his peppermint-flavored Yucatan Gum! The King graciously accepted it, and Bill cabled the news back to America. All the papers printed the story. This free publicity almost doubled the sale of his gum. Popcorn Bill had come a long way!

Enter William Wrigley.

From that point on, comparatively little change was made in the taste of chewing gum. But another name now enters the history: William Wrigley. Early in this century he went into the gum business and began pouring millions of dollars into advertising his Peppermint,

Spearmint and Juicy Fruit gums, all now so very familiar.

Juicy Fruit carries a hint of fresh fruit taste, actually imitation or synthetic, though people do not question it. But most people do not understand "Spearmint" as a brand name. Why "Spear"?

Spearmint is merely another kind of mint plant, named because the small flowers on their stems suggest little spears. Its flavor is only slightly different from that of regular mint plants. But "Spearmint" made a good advertising word. It seemed to lend an exotic touch to gum.

William "Bill" Wrigley became rich and famous. He not only developed delicious gums, he also improved their packaging. A package can make or break a product.

Metal foil, replacing waxed paper, was introduced as a wrapper for each of the five sticks in a Wrigley package. Then over the foil an attractively designed paper wrapper appeared in full color, with five sticks encased in yet another pretty paper wrapper.

Even then, the gum still tended to dry out too quickly and become hard to chew. The problem was solved when inexpensive plastic sheets—thin, strong and clear—came along. Wrigley's science experts wrapped the entire package in plastic, sealing the moisture in. With great pride they took a sample of it to Mr. Wrigley.

He accepted the new package, shiny and beautiful as if encased in glass. He picked at it with a fingernail. He twisted it a bit and clawed at it some more. Then he told his men, "It is very pretty, but where is the can opener?"

He could not get the tough plastic open! Small children would be frustrated, and they were the majority of

Wrigley customers. He could not risk losing them. So the experts went back to their brainstorming. They came up with a red pull-tab in the plastic. With a gentle pull, you had your five sticks of fresh, fragrant gum. This was a major advance. The can-opener tab is still in use.

Mr. Wrigley was loved as a kindly man and admired as a public citizen. In tribute to his son Philip K. Wrigley, a new gum package was created. Ten candy-coated tablets of gum, replacing the usual five sticks, were put into a small, flat box, all sealed in clear plastic and re-tailed for a nickel. The tablets were named "P K's" in honor of the son and became very popular. The candy coating enhanced their appeal.

A competitive product, almost identical in content and packaging but named "Chiclets," has dominated this particular market in many areas. These peppermint-coated gums are manufactured by Warner Lambert Pharmaceutical Company. Chiclets are made of a plastic base, starch, natural flavoring and that same corn syrup which proved to be a monumental discovery by Bill White many years before.

Competition!

Competition always arises when somebody produces a fast-selling item of merchandise. This has been true all through the years with chewing gum. Some gum brand names have been devised for special appeal. Dentyne, for example, is spiced with an extra amount of mint flavor, actually enough to sting the tongue a trifle, and is adver-tised as having a teeth-cleansing, mouth-freshening effect. Perhaps it really does combat bad breath, at least by providing a temporary odor that dominates the foul one. It also is colored red, which some merchants think improves its sales appeal.

In other areas of merchandising, especially among foods, red is the color with top customer appeal. For example, red delicious apples outsell the original yellow delicious species by about ten to one. Yellow-meat watermelon very often is sweeter than red-meat melon, but people rarely buy the yellow.

Surprisingly, in chewing gum red is *not* very desirable. Psychologists think that red suggests blood in the mouth. Many red gums offered experimentally have failed because of the color; our minds seem fixed on the unimpressive gray product. On the other hand, gum now marketed in slot machines in marble form has many red marbles which are quite popular. But the red is simply a candy coating for the usual gray gum and does not endure. Gum manufacturers have to outwit the public in its strange whims.

Since the year 1900, many gum brand names have come and gone. One early favorite was named "Kiss Me Gum," and was rather daring for that era. If a boy gave one to his sweetheart, a real kiss could result, and those with puritanical minds called him "fast." Such trivialities can have social significance.

The biggest overall change in gum in recent years has been the unpublicized switch from *sapodilla* chicle to the artificial tree sap, the plastic *polyvinyl acetate*. This was developed in World War II when the supply of tropical chicle was almost cut off. Fortunes were spent by the chewing gum industry in the 1940s looking for a substitute for chicle. A good substitute, *polyvinyl acetate*, was found and was cheaper to make than chicle had been to import. It was easier to control in mixing vats, more uniform in quality, better to chew, did no harm if swallowed, yet looked and tasted like real chicle gum.

Enemies of
Chewing Gum.

The growth of the chewing gum industry has not been smooth. Dating back to the days of General Santa Anna himself, there have been enemies of chewing gum. Many are still active.

Among the early enemies were the growers, processors and sellers of tobacco who indignantly said that tobacco—not tree sap—was the real American "chew." Thousands of men chewed tobacco in those years. Others used it in the form of ground powder called snuff. Foreign imported tree sap ought to be outlawed, the tobacco people insisted; it was unpatriotic and "sissy" to chew gum. Furthermore, the tobacco publicity men declared, sticky gum was not made from chicle tree sap, it was a mixture of glue and horses' hoofs. It sounds like a joke now; back then, it did not; it was taken very seriously, and people on both sides could speak with bitterness.

But tobacco had more enemies than chewing gum had. Chewing the tobacco weed, spitting and smelling and dribbling was a smelly, dirty habit. Gum chewing, on the other hand, was absolutely harmless.

The counter-campaign of propaganda soon caused tobacco people to retreat. They had lost the battle and knew it.

Other interesting enemies of gum popped up in the

early days. For example, some dentists declared that gum was likely to pull your teeth out if you chewed it. Or if you chewed too much, said a famous scientist named Nicola Tesla as recently as 1932, it would soon exhaust the salivary glands, causing your mouth to dry up completely, resulting in your death. Many doctors agreed, but there is as yet no instance of any such effect.

Other doctors warned that if a child should swallow a blob of gum it would cause the intestines to stick together, bringing certain death. This hasn't happened either. The doctors overlooked the fact that thousands of children had already swallowed their gum, with no apparent aftereffects.

Beginning with schoolrooms in the 1870s—and continuing with vigor even today—teachers have opposed gum-chewing by their students because they feel it distracts attention.

Again, there has been no measurable proof. A few teachers even feel that mild gum chewing in class is beneficial because it helps relax tensions so that the chewer can concentrate better. But there is no proof of that either.

Where to
Hide the Stuff!

A major problem is disposal of the gum after chewing. Dropped anywhere outside, it can "gum up the works" of a lawn mower, a walker's shoe, a dog's foot, a barefoot child's toes.

Most people slyly stick gum in school, at church, or in the movie theater somewhere out of sight, usually on the underside of chairs. Theater managers spend thousands of dollars cleaning used gum from the undersides of chair seats and sweeping up discarded gum wrappers. On the other hand, those same managers encourage the sale of gum—and candy, popcorn, cookies, ice cream and other goodies.

The manufacturers of gum did try to make us be thoughtful. A few years ago they printed on their packages, "Save this wrapper for disposal after use." That has been called the most ignored plea ever published. Tests showed that not one chewer in ten thousand did as requested. Even for those few who did, where and when would they dispose of the gum wrapped in its original paper? The problem has not been solved. Perhaps when we become more civilized . . . .

These problems have had no effect on gum's growing popularity. Canadians chew a lot of gum. People in the British Isles, New Zealand and Australia chew a lot of gum. Many people on the European mainland chew it, as do many in Africa, Asia and South America.

But gum chewing is primarily a phenomenon of the United States.

That Bubble.

Finally, we come to the bubble that balloons out of the mouths of youths.

Any kind of gum, whether chicle or plastic, has always been elastic and stretchy. The earliest chewers developed the habit of stretching the gum out with the tongue, retracting it with a slurping flourish of motion and sound, chewing a moment, then stretching it out again. More than a century ago manufacturers and merchants began studying that habit. Sometimes a child would gain prestige among his playmates by blowing out a small gum bubble an inch across.

The Frank H. Fleer Corporation of New York tried to cash in on the desire among children to "blow" their wads of gum. In 1885 it introduced a gum named "Blibber Blubber" and advertised that it could be blown.

It could, but the resulting small bubble was wet and too soft and splattered all over children's faces—to everyone's dismay. Bubble gum hadn't arrived yet.

Meanwhile, Frank Fleer's brother Harry, working in the Fleer laboratories, produced a new item. It was simply the usual chicle but made into a marble shape and coated with candy. Henry took some of the little balls to his brother. Frank was delighted with them. He declared that "Chiclets" was a good name and that the firm would put them on the market.

The candy-coated gum marbles were soon found in vending machines, selling for a penny each, sometimes two for a penny. The hard candy coating tended to keep the gum itself from drying out and getting too hard to chew. "Blibber Blubber" was abandoned so that the new "Chiclets" could be given every possible sales push. In time the Chiclets name and patent were sold to the American Chicle Company. Then after more time, Chiclets became the flat little candy-coated gum already referred to.

During those years, however, the Fleers never quite gave up on the thought of a really satisfactory bubble gum. Blibber Blubber had failed because it was too weak and sticky. What could possibly be done to make it strong and "dry?"

Big Bubbles.

In 1928 the Fleers found their answer. Their technicians produced a chicle compound that was almost rubbery. It was not the soft chew commonly enjoyed but was harder in texture, less tasty but more challenging. It gave exercise to the jaw muscles. Best of all—when spread across open lips and blown, out swelled balloons that might go up to four, six, eight, sometimes even twelve inches across.

By making the gum pink (not red), the bubble looked like a pretty balloon from a street carnival. It was better than the balloon, because when the gum exploded and disappeared, the pink goo could be chewed a bit and re-blown.

The result was sensational.

Here was a bubble gum that was *double* the strength of ordinary gum. By 1950 "Dubble Bubble" had swept across America, Canada, Europe, and everywhere gum was sold. It was not only a momentary bit of refreshing sweetness, then a lasting wad to chew, but it was also a toy. It ballooned and it lasted.

The Fleer people awaited any negative reaction. Surely somebody would find cause to criticize Dubble Bubble. Nobody did. In effect, parents threw up their hands in resignation; the bubbly stuff seemed harmless, however inelegant. Moreover, dentists and physicians now said that chewing and blowing it might help strengthen the jaw muscles and the whole mouth structure. The Fleer people couldn't have been happier.

Many true stories have been told concerning Dubble Bubble. American soldiers introduced it to Eskimos. These hardy Arctic ice dwellers promptly dropped their old habit of chewing whale blubber in favor of the new, pink, bubbly gum. It was prettier, less messy, more of a novelty.

Chapter 3

Breakfast Foods

A recent study was made at a large American supermarket. Its floor space was about the size of a football field. One corridor, with four-layer shelves 6 feet high and 90 feet long, held nothing but packaged breakfast foods. An inventory was taken. Many different varieties were displayed in highly colorful pasteboard boxes or plastic bags. Here are the brand names that were there:

Granada Bars (4 varieties)
Crunchola (5 varieties)
Carnation Breakfast Bar
  (6 varieties)
Maypo Oatmeal
Roman Meal (mixed cereals)
Wheat Hearts
Ralston Wheat Germ
Kretchmer Wheat Germ
Uncle Sam Cereal
Quaker Bran
Kellogg's Concentrate
Miller's Bran
Quaker Puffed Rice

Post Grape Nut Flakes
C. W. Post Family Style
  Cereal
Kix Crispy Corn Puffs
Oogles
Tasty Tips
Total
Buc Wheats
Yummies
Best Breakfast
Life
Kellogg's Frosted Flakes
Kellogg's Special K
Kellogg's Rice Crispies

Quaker Puffed Wheat
Post Fortified Oat Flakes
Post Raisin Bran
Post Grape Nuts
Dalite Delights
Motheraids
Janet Lee Corn Flakes
Kellogg's Corn Flakes
Kellogg's All Bran
Kellogg's Product 19
Peanut Butter Cereal
Kellogg's Cocoa Krispies
Nabisco 100% Bran
Peeky-Weekies
Choco Cereal
Wheaties
Sunnies
Shredded Wheathearts
Trix
Janet Lee Frosted Flakes
Crazy Cow
Lucky Charms
Dawn Food
Sweet 'N Neat
Wheatena
Malt-O Meal
Sugar Wheats
Fun Food
Bell Ringers
Corny-Snaps
Sugar Corn Pops
Country Morning
Frosty Tarts
Cocoa Pebbles

Nabisco Shredded Wheat
Morning Delight
Twinkies
Nabisco 100% Bran
Janet Lee Crispy Rice
Janet Lee Raisin Bran
Fun Favors
Kellogg's 40% Corn Flakes
Kellogg's Cracklin' Bran
Kellogg's Frosted Mini-
   Wheats
Rice Chex
Wheat Chex
Corn Chex
Grins & Smiles & Giggles &
   Laughs
Moonstones
Cream of Wheat
Cream of Rice
Cocoa Puffs
Count Chocula
Family Fare
Quaker Whole Wheat
Quaker Natural Cereal
Vita-Crunch
Sunrise Bites
Sparkies
Apple Jacks
Froot Loops
Frosted Rice
Pop Tarts
Alpha-Bits
Instant Breakfast (several
   kinds)

Super Sugar Crisp	Honeycomb
Toasty O's	Breakfast Squares
Cap'n Crunch	Cheerios

That's 97 trade names.

Not all of those trade names have been copyrighted. A few were purely local or regional, for testing. The supermarket was in a California town of about 30,000, but a similar market in Houston showed 128 trade names of breakfast cereal foods. Climate also is a factor; some brands sell better in Alaska than in Hawaii, and vice versa. Customs and habit patterns also affect sales. But everywhere there is a tremendous number of brand names. The inventory in California was made on a Monday morning. Next Monday, four of the brands were missing but seven new ones had been added. Asked about this, the store manager said, "It's awful. It's just too much of a good thing."

Promises, Promises.

You will recognize many of the names on the above list. Also you probably have been influenced by the intense national advertising used to sell them. The aggregate of this advertising is beyond measure. Every known medium is used—television, radio, newspapers, magazines and billboards all ding at you every day. The theme generally is an appeal to delicious taste, fun eating and good health. Frequently the text matter printed on the food containers promises you outright—or at least by strong implication—that if you eat *this* brand of breakfast food, you are bound to be healthier, stronger, happier, more appealing and charming, and generally more successful. The wording for this is very carefully devised and tested by experts in the advertising agency business hired by the food manufacturers. One president of a food corporation read the legend on his firm's newest container and exclaimed, "Heavens, I didn't realize that our stuff was *that* wonderful!"

In such instances, as in perhaps no other area of business, advertising agencies employ what is called exaggeration-for-emphasis: over-selling, stating the case too strongly. One result is what is called sub-juvenile technique. One TV commercial showed a handsome youth riding a surfboard in on a curling ocean wave while he spooned breakfast cereal into his mouth from a bowl, while grinning at us and saying, "My popularity is due to eating (name brand)." All around him hanging on that surfboard were beautiful girls, scantily clad, smiling and waving. That commercial was soon withdrawn; it was *too* preposterous.

The trade-name impact on all of us is so profound that sociologists are concerned by it. Somehow, common sense has to enter into our consideration and consumption of the brands. Exactly what is the *truth* about them?

One part of it is—these foods are not so bad, after all. They are composed primarily of four nourishing cereals—wheat, oats, barley and rice. Some have just one; others have all four or only two or three. Additives include almost anything from flaxseed and pecans to molasses and dried fruits. Seemingly, any mixture technicians can concoct, cook, and dry can be put into a glamorous package and sold under a catchy trade name.

The aggregate of those products form the major portion of what we call "junk" food. Junk meaning unworthy, misleading, gyp foods lacking in real value and likely to be harmful to the body.

That accusation is not fair. Some may have too much sugar but almost all the foods are at least acceptable. They are harmless because of strict government regulations. They are not all things to all people, but they do have reasonable food value. They will not make you gain weight any more than any other food, nor will they help you reduce. In short, the foods themselves are more honest than the advertising about them.

How Times Have Changed.

Specialized foods for breakfast began around 1910, when America was still primarily an agrarian (farming or ranching) nation. They grew in number, variety and popularity rather slowly, until about 1950, when they suddenly proliferated.

Since then packaged trade-name foods have multiplied like a plague of locusts. And the manufacturers use every conceivable trick to make us buy them. They offer prizes stuffed inside the boxes. They print coupons, saying that if you will send in four boxtops as proof of purchase, you can receive a gift by mail—if you also send perhaps 99 cents to pay cost of "handling and postage." This is all a part of modern merchandising technique.

Post Toasties.

A favorite breakfast cereal among young people today is one of the oldest—Post Toasties. Studies indicate this is because parents grew up on it. It has a catchy name, easy to remember.

Its history began in 1904 when a man named C. W. Post sensed the beginning national interest in specialized foods. He was already something of a nutritionist or food expert. So he devised a way of shaving grains of ordinary corn, flavoring them gently, and toasting them. This required much experimenting. But eventually he had a product which he thought tasted good, especially when served with cream and sugar.

So he packaged the flakes and labeled them *Elijah's Manna.*

Elijah, as you may know, was a character in The Bible. Manna was food from heaven itself. A good name, therefore, or so Mr. Post felt.

But America and Canada and Great Britain, where he sought to sell the product, were still religious minded, still into Victorian ethics. To his astonishment, Post had figuratively poked a stick into a hive of bees. Out swarmed the protestors, ready to sting!

From their pulpits and in print, ministers claimed that Mr. Post was guilty of blasphemy—of trying to use the Bible for personal gain. They were insulted and outraged. Post even had trouble getting *Elijah's Manna* registered as a trademark; Great Britain refused it outright.

Post hurriedly took *Elijah's Manna* off the market and waited until tempers cooled, then came out with the same product copyrighted as *Post Toasties.*

A simple, descriptive name, with no implications. Very soon, families began to be tempted by the advertising, and before anybody realized it, Post Toasties had become an American household term.

Post Toasties did not instantly replace heavier, traditional breakfasts. But it was accepted as a somewhat glamorous and sophisticated addition. Eating Toasties was a form of morning fun; its users felt modern. C. W. Post and his colleagues were delighted.

He Began in a Barn.

Mr. Post had started his research into foods on his parents' family farm near Battle Creek, Michigan, in 1895. What he called his laboratory was simply a room in the barn. Naturally, it made a good place for youths to hang out, and many helped him, as food tasters and testers.

Later, Mr. Post developed a disease which sent him into a sanitarium for several weeks, then forced him to stay in a wheelchair. Depressed and discouraged, he was unable to accomplish much for quite a while. But when he felt cured, he resumed his work on foods, and Post Toasties was just one of the results.

Another of his creations also became nationally known. It was a mixture of four cereals which he toasted brown, ground into a powderlike form, and marketed as a breakfast drink to replace coffee. Many people loved coffee, its taste and the relaxing, warming feel of it, yet were afraid it might be harmful. Some doctors preached against it.

Mr. Post's drink looked like coffee and had a vaguely similar taste, therefore it had strong psychological appeal. People took to it immediately. He named the product in honor of his own family—*Postum Cereal Food Coffee.*

That name proved to be not only a bit dishonest, but too long, too hard to remember and say. So, Mr. Post dropped the last three words of the trade name, and to-day the world still drinks *Postum* as a substitute for coffee. Recently, new competitors have been crowding it in sales with several brands of decaffeinated coffee. But Postum has its followers, along with Post Toasties.

Among other honors, a town is said to have been named in honor of C. W. Post—Post, Texas. C. W. himself used to visit there. One morning in the local hotel he came down to breakfast, and the eager waiter promptly set a cup of dark, steaming liquid before him.

Mr. Post tasted it, grimaced and demanded, "What is this stuff?" "That's Postum, sir," the happy waiter explained. "Your own fine breakfast drink." The distinguished guest gruffly said, "Take it away and bring me some coffee. Postum is made to sell, not to drink!"

It may or may not be a true story, but it does reflect the fact that not all trade names are sacrosanct.

Grape Nuts, Too.

Mr. Post's other major breakfast food, Grape Nuts, was a cereal mixture designed to be eaten cold with milk or cream. It had no grapes and no nuts in it. But its form was that of little pellets the size of grape seeds, and the taste had a hint of nutty flavor. For a while, each package of this cereal also carried a little pamphlet, written by Mr. Post. Its title was *The Road to Wellsville*. People were encouraged to think that if they ate a lot of Grape Nuts, they could get well from almost any ailment.

All in all, the C. W. Post story is fairly typical of hundreds which could be told about developers of "breakfast foods."

Chapter 4

Ketching Up
With Ketchup

Project yourself back to the first year of the 20th century. Make your way to what probably is the busiest, most publicized street intersection in the world, Times Square in New York City.

As always, it is surging with humanity, in a form of urban madness. You cannot hear yourself think. Dominant is the constant staccato roar of horses' hoofs on pavement, blending with the bumpity-bump of steel-rimmed wheels of wagons.

But through it all you hear a counterpoint. This is the new sound, the loud chug-chug-cough of the horseless carriage rolling down Broadway, sounding its raucous horn or tinklepinging its bell. You ignore its eye-stinging spurts of blue smoke, just as you ignore the stench of fresh manure, for the two are now an accepted part of urban life.

Times Square is a wondrous mixture of sounds and sights, with hundreds of wires strung high on the cross-arms of poles, and that revolutionary phenomenon, the electric light.

The area is much more crowded than usual. As you

stand there gawping, there is a sudden, loud cheer from the multitude because, suddenly, on a steel frame extending six stories high, the world's first electric sign comes alive.

In huge letters twinkling under the picture of a giant cucumber pickle, the sign says:

HEINZ
57 VARIETIES

Today you would scarcely notice such a thing. Then, it was not only an electrical marvel, it proclaimed a new business on the American scene, destined to touch almost every family and individual. Heinz. Today, many decades later, it is a national household term.

Born for
The Ministry.

Heinz is a Germanic family name, pronounced with a long-i sound and rather abruptly—*hintz*, not hin-z-z-z-z.

Many families named Heinz migrated to young America, one settling in Sharpsburg, Pennsylvania.

Henry Heinz was born there in 1884. His religious parents planned to educate young Henry as a clergyman. They dreamed that he would become a fine orator, preaching in a big church. But necessity, circumstance, environmental influences or fate often upsets parents' planning. The small boy Henry read his Bible right enough, but when time came to study for the ministry, Mrs. Heinz found she needed help with the farm. She drafted her eldest son, Henry.

After a few months, young Hank decided that while he

had nothing against the religious vocation, delicious fresh apples, blackberries, peas and corn somehow came first. He was perhaps more physical than spiritual.

At age twelve Henry was driving an open hack—forerunner of our pickup truck—along residential streets calling out to housewives—"FRESH VEGE-TABLES, RIGHT OUT OF OUR GARDEN, NEW CORN TODAY. FRESH VEGE-TABLES, TENDER UND SVEET MIT TASTEN GUT."

Everyone beamed on him—a dear boy, with an infectious grin, a charming German accent, and truly delicious garden produce. They bought from him.

At age sixteen he was peddling his garden produce wholesale to grocers in the city of Pittsburgh. Again he was successful, and the alert mid-teen businessman had young people working for him as helpers.

But a financier must be versatile; he has to be on the lookout for better investments. At age nineteen Henry Heinz thought he saw better opportunity as manager of an ice-making plant. He quit gardening and took the executive job.

But that winter nature froze everything to crystal hardness. Ice could be cut free and stored cheaper than manufactured ice could be delivered. Henry Heinz got fired.

Feeling depressed and a failure, he moped around for a few days, despairing of his future. But he did own a wagon and a team of horses, so finally he took his emotions in hand, approached a farmer and talked him into selling a load of fresh spring vegetables on credit. He turned his wagon homeward and again raised the cry of "FRESH VEGE-TABLES" at household doors. When he unhitched at the home barn in Sharpsburg, his wagon was empty but his pocket was not. He had enough money to send full payment to the farmer who had helped him and proudly showed his parents a $25 profit. The life juices were streaming inside young Henry Heinz again; confidence had returned.

For the next few years one thing led to another as he ventured more and more into the produce business. He took up with a pleasant, honest companion named L. C. Noble, and together they got into the sale of horseradish.

Frontier people learned long ago to grate this root and use it as a relish to spread on meats. It seemed especially delicious when toned down with cream and eaten with roast beef. That opinion still holds today.

Henry the gardener knew all about horseradishes. So he and his new friend along with his friend's brother organized the Heinz and Noble Company, to raise horseradishes. The boys gathered and planted nearly an acre of it. This was like overplanting of tomatoes—one vine will supply fruits for a family, but home gardeners commonly set out a long row of them, then have so many tomatoes they can't even give them away. Henry Heinz should have known better, but his enthusiasm was the enemy of caution. In due time he and young Noble had horseradish coming out of their ears.

First of the 57.

So the boys made horseradish into the tangy spread which was to become the first of the 57 Varieties.

They worked hard gathering, washing, grating and bottling their relish by hand, then peddling it. Happily, horseradish was already known, so they needed no educational campaign such as many new brand-name products have required. In fact, there were many crude but enjoyable jokes about it, just as there are today. "Aw, horseradish!" a teenager might exclaim at somebody pulling his leg in an outrageous statement of any kind. Or if somebody told a tall tale, listeners in a chorus might dismiss him by rumbling "Aw, horseradish," just as "Aw baloney" came to connote the same kind of put-down in the 20th century. Horseradish is *violent*. The so-called practical joker often employed white horseradish. It would be undetected—until the victim took a big bite, in vanilla ice cream at a birthday party.

After about two years of horseradish sales, Heinz and Noble Company expanded. They hired help and added "Variety No. 2" to their line of merchandise—celery sauce.

This had nowhere near the appeal of horseradish, but it did carry its own weight. Then very soon, with the gears of his brain meshing smoothly, Henry remembered the wonderful cucumber pickles he enjoyed as a child. "Variety No. 3" became the cucumber pickle. Everybody loved it; friends were honored to get a bottle of Heinz and Noble pickles.

Events began to move fast now. Henry and his partner acquired 100 acres of rich land, hired help and began planting fields of vegetables. Bottling and sales zoomed; prosperity sat on their desks. The boys went out to farmers and signed contracts to buy total crop outputs. But then a financial panic and depression swept America in the 1870s. When harvest time came the crops were superabundant and fine, but money had evaporated. The company went bankrupt. Henry could not even buy his young wife Sally a Christmas gift.

Then Sally raised some money on a piece of property she owned. She, his mother Anna, his brother John and cousin Frederick, all chipped in and came up with $3,000—a small fortune for that era. Henry could not own a share of the company at this point because of his bankruptcy. He went to work for the new F. and J. Heinz Company, used his parents' home as a packing plant, and went back into the business of making food for the dining tables of America.

What's In a Name?

At this point the greatest, most popular, most maligned, most laughed at, most sold and enjoyed of all food helpers was developed. The Heinz firm began to grow tomatoes and convert them into—

Ketchup?
Ketch-up?
Catchup?
Catsup?
Catsop?

What's in a name? The answer has to be—almost everything. A name can make or break any product. Manufacturers, growers, advertising agencies and publicity experts all team up, straining to come up with good names that the public will accept and which will motivate it to buy.

You well know what tomato ketchup is. You know how we pound the bottom of the bottle and none of the r~ '

gooey stuff comes out at first; then—*swoosh*—too much
will burst out.

This tomato-stuff originated not in America but somewhere in or around Singapore. A century before Henry
Heinz was born, sailors had brought it to America. Then
it was called *kechap*. We cannot now be sure just which
Asiatic language gave us that name for the condiment,
nor does it matter. What mattered was, and is—it en-
hances the flavor appeal of meats and other foods. It was
very popular in England around the year 1750; both
Dickens and Lord Byron praised it in their writings. It is
astounding to see the many uses to which it is now put.
Everyone "bops the bottle" over French fried potatoes,
potato chips, steaks, cuts of pork, chicken, hamburgers,
fish, soups, and almost anything that comes to the table.
There is just something about the mild tangy taste of tomato ketchup which has been worth millions of dollars to
Henry Heinz and his heirs.

One of the wealthiest men America ever produced,
William Randolph Hearst, bought a large, beautiful
castle in Europe and had every stone, statue, tapestry, table, and chair shipped to a hilltop in a picturesque California wilderness and reassembled. Mr. Hearst called his
castle San Simeon. Celebrities, renowned actors, musi-
cians, and politicians were his guests there. The dinner
table was set with the finest sterling silver, exquisite imported china, handmade linen napkins and table cloth,
and flower bowls, everything lavish. Naturally, the food
was in keeping—only the very best.

But at his orders, the waiters placed two or three
cheap, store-bought bottles of Heinz ketchup right there

in all that luxury. Hearst said that bopping the bottle was a sacred American ritual, and he was right.

Henry Heinz and his family began to bottle and sell ketchup. The red color was in its favor; everyone liked red; other food sauces are black or brown, and while they have fine taste appeal, they nowhere near approach the sales of red tomato ketchup. Experiments with yellow tomatoes for ketchup failed also. Henry was delighted with his discovery. It boosted the firm into high prosperity, and he began studying the potential for expansion.

One day on a New York train Henry saw a signboard advertising shoes. It said "21 styles." And he sat there click-clacking over the rails, his mind began to doodle with that sign. If one shoe manufacturer could offer 21 styles, one condiment manufacturer could offer many styles of foodstuffs.

But *How* Many?

At this moment, the firm already had more than 60 items on the market; various kinds of mustards, peppers, salts, pickles, and sauces, with more constantly being added. Should he count them and offer, say, "75 styles"? No. "Style" was the wrong word. He felt that "variety" would be better. How many varieties should he proclaim, then?

For several hours on the train he kept on doodling with pencil on paper, quietly brainstorming the idea of a trade slogan for advertising purposes. *Seven* seemed to him a sort of magic number. He wasn't sure why, it was merely an intuitive feeling. *Five* was considered a good number, too.

Finally he decided arbitrarily on 57 varieties, no matter how many the firm really had. He liked the looks and sound of it. So when he got into New York City he immediately ordered a big advertising campaign based on "Heinz 57 Varieties." He ruled out use of any other words, such as pickles, ketchup, sauce. Let the people wonder what the slogan meant. Sound psychology.

You know the rest. In 1900 the big, six-story electric light flashed into brilliance in New York City, showing the slogan and a picture of a pickle above it.

Since then the slogan has become a household term everywhere. When Henry Heinz died in 1918, his company already had 7,000 employees and he himself had become immensely wealthy from his garden products reduced to bottled forms.

If the dog in our back yard is a mutt, we call it a "Heinz," because of its multi-varieties; if the flower bed is an old-fashioned kind with petunias, asters, carnations, tulips and other blossoms, we say that 57 varieties are showing. If we see many kinds of anything, we are likely to use the term.

Henry Heinz would have loved us for that.

Chapter 5
Bob, The Cold-Minded

Strange things happen to people. Often there is no accounting, no logical reason, for them; they simply develop in the march of events. But they often turn out individuals whose influence somehow sprouts, takes root, then grows nationally and even worldwide, touching the lives of uncounted millions.

That happened to an unknown fellow whose first name was Clarence, which was sometimes held unjustly to be a sissy name for a boy. Clarence therefore adopted the nickname Bob. He had a surname, but we will get to that later when you can better appreciate its impact on your personal life. Clarence—Bob— was a sensitive, small lad. Shy, but brilliant, he could never have dreamed of the indelible mark he would leave on business history. But he created one of the dozen or so greatest trade names ever known. Though long dead, he indirectly touches your life once or twice every day.

Rat Catcher!

Straining to make something of himself, Bob started in

business by catching rats. Bob learned that the science
department of Columbia University (in New York City)
would pay him a nickel each for live rats to be used in experiments. A nickel had some dignity back there around
the turn of the century.

So he became a rat trapper. And, expanding his
animal-catching enterprise, he also began to collect frogs
for the Bronx Zoo, which used them as food for certain
aquatic animals.

As he grew into his teens and young adulthood, Bob
left home on a trek into the Southwest. He took to the
picturesque region called Arizona and New Mexico, and
began collecting ticks—those repulsive creepie-crawlies
that latch onto human or animal flesh, suck blood and
cause diseases. Bob was a budding scientist, and was
making an important study of spotted fever, caused by
certain ticks.

In many areas of the Southwest wilderness, you can
ride a horse for a whole day and not encounter another
human being. In Bob's time, the population was almost
frighteningly sparse, but he did encounter a few professional trappers. From them he bought the hides of coy-
otes, bobcats, pumas, sometimes a bear, and rattlesnakes.
These he could sell either for scientific study or as tro-
phies and souvenirs. It was a way to help earn a living
while he was learning. He thought he might live all his
life in the sun-kissed, arid territory.

Moving Northward.

But a colder destiny awaited him.

Something lured him away up into Michigan, where

ponds freeze over and snowstorms roar. Up there he began to trap timber wolves. He would walk nearly 100 miles a week, following his trap lines. We can surmise that Bob was something of a loner but also an adventurer.

In Michigan Bob began to develop an unusual interest in *cold*. Winter, he well knew, could be an enemy; it has massive power. How could some of that power be harnessed and put to good use? Such is the nature of a scientist's inquiring mind, and in Bob's mind an idea was germinating.

At age 26, circumstance enabled him to meet Sir Wilfred Grenfell of England, who was sailing a famous hospital ship to Labrador. Bob promptly signed on as a jack-of-all-trades. The cold world in Labrador fascinated him, so he jumped ship, purchased a team of huskies and a sled, and set out alone to explore that icy region.

He almost froze to death, but he also collected enough pelts of sea animals to sell for $6,000 when he got back to civilization. With all that money in pocket, he decided to head back south, and ended up in the nation's capital.

Among the first people he met there, in 1915, was a young lady named Eleanor Gannett. Never one to dilly-dally around, he moved fast. Eleanor was impressed by this handsome young adventurer. The two of them married and headed back to Labrador with their new baby. A very young threesome, adventuring. But Bob also had a job as a fish and wildlife surveyor for the United States Government.

His work took them into the ice-covered wilderness so that the family was out of touch with normal food supplies. Often they had to subsist on whatever fish he could catch. They badly needed fresh vegetables.

Once on a trip to a seaport, he purchased a big crate of fresh cabbages shipped up from the States and took them back to his icy home. But the family could eat only one cabbage a week. How to preserve the others?

Bob put them in a barrel and covered them with sea water, which promptly froze solid. For months afterward, Eleanor had only to chop out a frozen cabbage, thaw it, cook it, and the family could enjoy it in its preserved freshness.

And right there is where *Birds Eye Frozen Foods* were born!

Clarence "Bob" Birdseye will live in food history forever. He not only created the trade name, he revolutionized the business of preserving fresh vegetables, fruits, meats, and complete precooked dinners.

Bob of course didn't discover deep-freezing, he simply adapted it. Around the world for centuries, edible foods have been kept for months by freezing with natural ice or frigid air.

Bob's contribution was that his idea was timed right. It came when the processes of making artificial cold and ice were being perfected. Bob had the wit to capitalize on this. The Birds Eye saga (Bob's name was divided later for trademark purposes because it was easier to read) now ranks high among the legends of business and industry.

Bobby Birdseye used his discovery about cabbages to begin freezing fish. By 1923 he was head of a firm called Birdseye Seafoods, Inc., with headquarters in New York

City. He prospered quickly, yet a problem arose; he could not get enough production fast enough.

The Ice Man.

The ice house was once a standard fixture on every town's business scene. Ice houses had their deep vats of water in compartments holding several hundred pounds, surrounded by pipes of refrigerant, plus a lot of rather crude machinery for pumping, lifting, sliding, and loading. From those factories, the ice man started his rounds of the town each morning.

In summer the ice man often was a strong high school or college student who owned or leased a flatbed, horse-drawn hack, which may or may not have had a shade cover on it. He would put several hundred-pound blocks of ice on the back, then make old Dobbin trot down residential streets. Dobbin learned to stop automatically at the home of the Smiths, the Joneses, and the McGillicuddys. The ice man would pick up heavy iron tongs, snap them onto a 50- or 100-pound block, turn his back and shoulder the ice. Bowed, he would lumber through the kitchen door and noisily plop his ice into a large insulated box. Woe to the customer if the icebox had not been cleared for the twice-weekly refill. Likely as not, the ice man would also be invited to help himself—he was a break in the morning routine.

But the ice merely chilled. It could be crushed and mixed with rock salt, and used to freeze a gallon of ice cream fixings, but that was the limit of its freezing capacity. No other foods could be frozen in the icebox which just kept things partially fresh and safe for a few days at most.

For one thing, the ice was too hot. Yes, *hot*! Not all ice has the same temperature. Water freezes at zero degrees Celsius. But those commercial blocks were, and still are, much colder. However, as old Dobbin hauled it around town, the temperature of the ice rose from maybe minus 20 Celsius to minus 5 or 2. And it kept warming up in the icebox.

Bob Birdseye knew that he needed dependable, stable, far-below-zero temperatures and he needed *instant* freezing at low expense. So, scientist that he was, he developed it. He had a Source Mind—if he faced a technical problem, he put his brain to it and usually came up with a solution.

Food tissues tend to break down when ice crystals take over slowly, and much of the food's nutritional value is lost. In quick freezing, the ice crystals take hold instantly and hold the food unchanged. So Mr. Birdseye developed what came to be called the *belt freeze*. Packaged foods were put on a belt, rolled through a really deep cold zone, and came out hard as a rock at sub-zero temperature. This was the technical process which solved his problem.

"Will It Poison Us?"

The next big problem was to get suspicious consumers to accept quick-frozen foods. He had been encouraged by a few restaurants and individuals. But most people didn't like the idea of any meat or vegetable that was weeks old, frozen or not. They were afraid it would poison, even kill them.

Knowing about this natural reluctance, Bob Birdseye launched a national educational campaign. As always, some people did accept what they were told and tested deep-frozen food. They not only survived but remained in good health. Much talk arose. Amateur and professional comedians made jokes about deep-freezing. Girls who were not responsive to a pass were said to be deep-frozen. If a girl wanted to get rid of a boy who was pressing his attentions, she "gave him the deep freeze," with protective haughty looks and manner. Deep freeze entered the language.

Clarence Birdseye aged along, and he finally sold his interest for about $1 million to one of those great corporate structures now called conglomerates. Birdseye Frozen Foods became a division of General Foods. The popularity of his products kept growing. Even the American Medical Association—a group often reluctant to accept new developments—finally declared that Bob's quick-frozen foods were wholly good and safe. Even the vaunted vitamins were largely retained.

Go, now, and thaw out something for lunch or dinner. And give a passing thought to Clarence Birdseye.

Chapter 6

The Romance of "Sally Rate-Us"

You have probably spent considerable time today at your favorite occupation—eating. If you did, you almost certainly ate something named *saleratus*.

You enjoyed it, perhaps unknowingly. It is kind of sneaky. It stays hidden. In fact you don't know it's there, although you miss it acutely when it isn't. You probably never use the correct word for it, and cannot now define it. Saleratus is a rather harsh and definitely unpleasant-tasting chemical compound. So why would good cooks put it into meals? Is it all that important?

It is. You would not enjoy eating many foods if saleratus were missing: crackers, for instance, that you eat with your soup or with cheese.

It is *so* important to you and everyone else that the principal name under which it is marketed has long been one of the dozen brand names most favored by English-speaking people.

More than a century ago, the word itself, as well as the product, became legendary. Shortly before the Civil War, young people made jokes about "Miss Sally Rate-us." "Whom are you taking to the picnic?" somebody might ask a young man. To which the young and smiling Man-About-Town would airily reply, "Sally Rate-us, of course. We make a good team."

At that time, saleratus was primarily a Northern product, just getting to be known in the less populous South. But it soon became a good seller in the Confederate states, and its name entered the folklore of the War. A Southern camp song of the War years said that:

> The Yankees live away up North
> And they have learned to hate us.
> But I will march myself up there
> And marry Sally Rate-us.

It was a song of defiance, with prized but hard-to-get *baking soda* as a symbol.

Baking soda—ordinary kitchen pantry stuff—saleratus was, and still is; simple sodium bicarbonate, or bicarbonate of soda. But today it is marketed primarily under a famous symbol, a label that has become one of the most famous trade names of all time.

Right now, it probably is just a taken-for-granted item on the pantry shelf, usually in the traditional yellow pasteboard box. It goes into the biscuit dough. A pinch of it in water will help peas retain their appealing green color. Alone, it tastes horrid, yet people mix it with water to use as a gargle and mouthwash. A little bit mixed dry with a pinch of salt in the palm of the hand makes an ideal powder for brushing teeth.

Saleratus—soda—also can serve as an emergency fire extinguisher. Throw a handful of it quickly on a flare-up of flame from a frying pan and the fire is out immediately. Moisten a bit and paste it on a mosquito bite and the itch recedes. Dust some on a fruit stain, and the color may be bleached out. An open box in the refrigerator eliminates odors. Many kinds of bread and cake doughs "rise" when a bit of soda generates gas in the dough. But drink a little soda dissolved in water, and it may prevent or alleviate gas on the stomach.

The one renowned, favored trade name for baking saleratus is *Arm & Hammer Soda*.

All brands of baking soda are the same. But we are interested in the true stories behind famous brand names. This strange one ranks high. Strange? Of course it is. What does an *arm* and a *hammer* have to do with a chemical?

There is no sure way to understand the psychology of trade names, no way to anticipate whether the public will accept or reject any one of them. This makes marketing a major financial gamble.

Jim Church's
Vulcan Spice Mill.

So then, let us explore the reasons for *Arm & Hammer's* astounding success.

The story begins when a young man named Jim Church set out to make a living for himself in Brooklyn in the middle of the 19th century. He had already enjoyed some experience in the grocery business, so he opened a little store which he named "The Vulcan Spice Mill."

There, he offered mustard and an assortment of exotic spices brought in from around the world. This included the ever-cherished black pepper—ground coarse or fine, or in the original seed state called "peppercorns." He offered red pepper, too, and ginger and cinnamon, curry, thyme, cloves, mace, oregano, rosemary, sassafras and assorted "yarbs" (herbs) of local origin, anything that would make foods more enjoyable and nourishing. It must have been a very aromatic store, if not a very large one.

We do not know just why Jim Church named his store the Vulcan Spice Mill. Again we say, whim alone sometimes dictates the naming of products and businesses. Vulcan would seem to have nothing whatever to do with spices. Vulcan is a character in mythology, a god of metalworking and fire, a god with a powerful arm and heavy hammer. At any rate, the Vulcan Spice Mill did well in Civil War times.

Actually, the mid-19th century was a physical era, when a man's powerful physique, especially the bulging bicep muscles, was regarded as a symbol of achievement and grandeur. All boys yearned to have such strength.

Jim Church hung a sign over the door of the Vulcan Spice Mill that simply showed a man's powerful right arm bent at the elbow and holding the handle of a heavy iron hammer. It was right and proper for its time; an apt choice, good public relations.

"Sally."

By 1867, baking soda (still generally called saleratus) was coming into its own. Demand for it grew rapidly. Alert Mr. Church took notice; he saw saleratus as the Coming Thing. So he decided to strike while the iron was hot—an

apt phrase, considering his Vulcan trade name and his
Arm & Hammer trademark.

The Vulcan Spice Mill disappeared and a new store
was opened under the name of Church and Company.
Jim Church, guided perhaps by sentiment, hung the
same arm-and-hammer painting over the door of the new
business establishment. If it had no direct relation to a
chemical that made better bread, so what? The arm-and-
hammer sign was already well ingrained into the con-
sciousness of Jim's customers.

In those days, saleratus was manufactured in chemical
plants and packaged in big barrels for distribution to retail stores. A grocer could thus buy a waist-high barrel of
the white powder, then dish it out in whatever sized par-
cels cooks might want. Each distributor would send along
a supply of paper sacks for the retailer's convenience.
Many varied brand names, with garish illustrations, were
imprinted on those sacks. The pictures and names tended
to run to flowers: *Lily* brand saleratus, for example, with
a pretty blossom showing.

Very often, too, saleratus was peddled from door to
door in cities, towns and villages. This was a common
practice with many items of merchandise. In fact, the
peddler was a major personage on the American scene
from Civil War time until about 1910. But Jim Church
stuck generally to wholesale and retail store sales.

Treetop Tall!

Jim Church decided he needed advertising to beat his
competition.

With his instinctive flair for showmanship, his romantic nature and imagination, Jim hired a giant. Literally that. The fellow stood seven-feet-four. He was called "Treetop" Powell and reputedly had been an Army Colonel. Perhaps he really had been, but in post-Civil War years, on into the 20th century, it seemed as if almost every ex-soldier had held the rank of Colonel. At any rate, Colonel Treetop Powell was a commanding figure of a man, made more so by the wearing of high-heeled boots and a high stovepipe hat which topped off at well over eight feet. He took over the job of promoting and advertising Church and Company "Arm & Hammer" saleratus.

We do not know exactly when "saleratus" became "soda" in public usage. Strictly speaking, soda is the common term used not only for sodium bicarbonate, but for sodium carbonate, sodium hydroxide, sodium oxide, and soda water. Unofficially, however, "soda" for saleratus seems to have evolved simultaneously but separately with soft drinks called soda water because they fizzed whenever a bottle was opened—saleratus when dissolved in water also bubbled or fizzed.

Anyhow, the American people came up with "soda" for the white powdery sodium bicarbonate, and by degrees ARM & HAMMER SODA also emerged on the national scene.

Treetop-tall Colonel Powell rode about the countryside promoting the product. Naturally, such a personage dominated any gathering. He had only to leave his saddle or his buggy for a crowd to gather. Gawking people would follow him into any store. There, with a smile and an eloquent speech, he would tack an Arm & Hammer Soda sign to the ceiling—while he stood on the floor. He would flex his powerful right arm while holding a heavy hammer, gesticulating with it to emphasize points in praise of his product. He was better than the wandering medicine shows, whose phony "doctors" sold useless cure-alls at outrageous prices.

Just about everyone came to recognize the Arm & Hammer sign, which became worth millions of dollars to Church and Company.

Today, well over a century later, it is the Church and Dwight Company. But the dominance of the trade name still holds; the muscular arm still hoists the hammer inside the red-and-white circle on the yellow box of baking soda.

Chapter 7
From Psalms 45:8

This true business story began more than a century ago at Cincinnati, Ohio. A boy approaching manhood was working at a factory where certain chemicals were blended and made ready for sale to American households. One day he was in charge of a large vat filled with smelly, gooey stuff, which a crude machine was slowly mixing. Noon came. He decided that the machine could just go on turning, doing its work while he went off to lunch.

He "goofed off," staying much longer than usual. The mixer was still slowly turning when he returned, making business history, creating something that touches life even a century later.

The young man's machine paddles were mixing a vat of toilet soap. But due to his prolonged lunchtime, the batch was overly mixed. When he poured the soap into the molds that formed hand-sized bars, he discovered that the bars were not up to standard weight. The over-mixing had filled the soap with an extra amount of air.

The young man was frightened. If the boss discovered his negligence, he would surely be fired. Hoping it might pass unnoticed, he went ahead and packaged the too-light bars, and shipped them all out of the factory to be sold in retail stores. He fervently hoped that he could get by with his dishonesty, that nobody would notice the slightly lighter weight of this one shipment.

He did *not* escape detection. A few days after the shipment went out, orders began to pour in from retail stores demanding "more bars of the white soap that floats." All soap in that era was heavy, much heavier than water—soap could not possibly float.

But this one batch of bars did, and its ability to float made it much more desirable in the customers' estimation. They liked seeing it on top of the water instead of slithering out of reach to the bottom of the tub. One customer wrote, "I bathe in our pond, and this floating soap is a great help there." A lady wrote, "My little son sticks a sail on his bar and has a tiny boat to play with in the tub."

**The Villain
Became A Hero.**

The manufacturers were dumbfounded. They called in the young man who told of the extra stirring, and to his utter astonishment he was made a hero, and given a raise in pay. We do not have a record of the careless young workman's name. He was just one of several employees at Proctor & Gamble, a chemical corporation that manufactured soap.

A small thing, yes; but historic in the world of business. Many such accidents or unplanned developments have changed the whole course of operations and sales.

By now you know which soap it was; you know its name.

Since then, the nation has been told millions of times that "it floats." A great fortune was built around that fact.

For many years, the few high-quality toilet soaps had been of the refined white color originally made in the city of Castile, Spain. Their principal ingredients were olive oil and sodium hydroxide. In rural America, harsher soaps were made by using wood ashes as a basis for obtaining lye and mixing it with a form of animal fat. The homemade stuff was very harsh and hard on human flesh, although it served well in laundering clothes. Many thousands of homes had no other, from pre-Revolutionary times into the early 1900s. In some areas it is still made today.

The crude lye soap was an ugly yellowish-brown and smelled horrid. The new white, "Castile" type from Proctor & Gamble was much more delicate, refined, and more generally desirable. In an era when the art of public relations and advertising was just dawning, the company announced that their product—called simply The White Soap—not only floated, but was "pure."

But how does one define "pure"?

An unabridged Webster's Dictionary lists twenty synonyms for "pure," such as clear, simple, genuine, real, undefiled. It defines "pure" as meaning free from anything that adulterates, taints or impairs.

So how could all those wonderful attributes apply? Surprisingly, the public got interested; people began to talk about The White Soap. Seemingly they decided that it really was pure, hence its sales increased rapidly.

Young Harley Proctor, half of the firm, began to explore the possibilities for further promoting sales of his floating soap. It was he who had ordered extra air mixed into all the White Soap his factory produced. The soap was riding a wave of word-of-mouth publicity created by the fact that it would float, and profits were increased because the soap ingredients were stretched.

Under its uninspired name, The White Soap, Harley Proctor's product was already doing fine, but he sensed greater possibilities. He had professors of chemistry analyze the soap. They verified that it was indeed as nearly "pure" as he could hope for. It held no foreign or useless substance.

Harley Proctor wanted to imply perfection in his fine soap without actually claiming it. Such a claim would only cause a negative reaction in the public. But how much should he claim? Eighty, ninety percent?

Finally he decided on *99 and 44/100 percent pure*, and that has become one of the most thoroughly approved and accepted advertising slogans ever known. Psychologically it was sound; it admitted to just a *little* imperfection—such as each of us will admit to in ourselves—but not enough to be worth consideration. The public responded by buying millions of bars, a process continuing here a century later.

**But A Better
Name Was Needed.**

As you may have guessed, Harley Proctor then went one step further in his reach for good public relations. He realized that the old name "White Soap" was about as im-

aginative and glamorous as a brickbat. All it did was proclaim whiteness against the ugly, smelly old lye soap.
Now it needed romantic appeal.

He became almost obsessed with his search. Often he
stared off at clouds, thinking and daydreaming. How
about "Cloud Soap" as a name? Clouds generally were
clean and pure and white. Or "Fleecy Soap" might do.
No, fleece suggested sheep more than clouds, he decided.
Still searching, he considered "Ocean Spray Soap"
named for the eternal white breakers and foam on the
beaches. They even made suds there. Not bad, not bad at
all! He was tempted. Ocean spray was cleansing and
white and beautiful, all fine connotations. On the other
hand, most people did not live at a seashore, so were not
ocean-minded enough to respond to such a name. By
such mental writhings and strainings, hundreds of trade
brand names have been evolved.

One Sunday Harley went to church as usual. During
the quiet prayers, his mind wandered off to his problem
of finding a soap name. But he snapped back to dutiful
attention when the pastor stood up and read the Bible
text for that day. It just happened to be Psalms 45:8:

> All thy garments smell of myrrh, and aloes, and cassis,
> out of the ivory palaces, whereby they have made thee
> glad.

Harley was inspired.

As soon as the final prayer dismissed the congregation,
he hurried to his buggy and drove to his office, not even
pausing to have lunch.

On a sheet of paper, in bold flourishes, he sketched in

these words which all the English-speaking world now
recognizes:

IVORY SOAP

99 and 44/100 percent pure.

Chapter 8

Your "Permanent" Beauty

It would be no exaggeration to say that every woman has yearned to be at least pretty, and if possible, beautiful. Similarly, men dream of being handsome. Since few of us are satisfied with what we have, we want to change our looks. Hair revisions—cuttings, thinnings, shapings, stylings—are a major concern.

Somehow, *curly* hair, or at least wavy hair, on both males and females, has usually been adjudged more desirable than straight hair.

Having to force-curl hair every day or for every special social function has always been a nuisance. Therefore scientists began centuries ago trying to find some way for us to make ringlets, curls, waves or whatever stay in our hair, once put there. Eventually, someone succeeded: Karl Ludwig Nessler.

Karl Nessler developed the trade name, *The Permanent*, for his process of permanent waving. Unfortunately for Nessler, he could not or did not patent his process or copyright the name.

Technically, of course, there is no such thing as a really *permanent* wave; the hair grows out in a few months—straight again. But Karl's name was a good one.

Hair Curling
Is Ancient.

To understand Karl Nessler's achievement we need some background knowledge.

Perhaps our early ancestors had thick hair all over their bodies; we have vestigial proof of that. Hair was physical protection from heat and cold and blows. But somewhere back in time we began to protect ourselves further by covering most of our bodies with skins and fabrics. This lessened the need for bodily hair, and most of it gradually receded.

The hair on our heads served a decorative rather than protective function. At least 4,000 years ago in Egypt, men were heating irons with which to curl their handsome beards and head hairs; we have no proof that women curled their hair. We haven't really improved on Egyptian man's technique very much; we still have to heat irons to roll our hair in order to create wavy "Permanents." Ancient Grecians thought that wavy hair was more beautiful than straight hair; marble statues prove it. Ringlets or large curls were in fashion when Nero played his fiddle as he watched Rome burn.

Later, in the Old World, an era called The Dark Ages came along, and people seemed to forget all about curling their straight hair. Perhaps they were just too depressed to care how they looked. It was hard times. The imperative was to survive, not make oneself beautiful. But that era melded gradually into an upturn of spirits and achievements called the Renaissance, the renewal, in which curling hair came back into vogue. Metal workers who hammered out swords, suits of armor and shields, also trained apprentices to make little irons that could be heated to curl hair. This took place in Italy, Spain, France and elsewhere.

Perhaps you have heard of "perukes." They are still worn in British courts by judges and barristers. A peruke is a wig, usually in long, down-to-the-shoulders design, and made of curled hair, normally white. It caught the fancy of ladies and male dandies in the 1700s, in both Europe and the American Colonies. During that long stretch of years, hair dressing became a major art in the field of costuming and grooming.

Queen Victoria came to the throne of Great Britain when that country dominated the world in military, cultural and fashion-setting power. Her Majesty did not care for most of the folderol attending hair styles. Curls? Not for Victoria. She went in for the severe bun, tightened from straight hair. What we in the 1970s named the "fall" in hair styling became fairly common among young girls back then in Great Britain, then in other countries, including the United States.

But in the same era, the French were experimenting with hair styles. Victoria's influence faded; her subjects, and the American people, were influenced by a fellow in Paris named Marcel. Marcel popularized a hair-do which became known as The Marcel Wave, not curls, but flat waves. The Marcel Wave is mostly forgotten now; back then, it was a major sensation. But its set would last only a few hours; the next night you would have to get your wave set in again. And the cost was high.

Enter the Hero.

In the same second half of the nineteenth century, in a cottage located in the picturesque Alps of Bavaria, Karl Ludwig Nessler was born.

His father was a shoemaker, straining to eke out a living for his family. Karl was the baby of the family. Largely ignored by the older children, he became a bookworm.

Karl earned a bit of money tending sheep. He developed an interest in their hair: it dawned on him that whereas his own naturally curly hair tended to straighten out in rain, the hair of the sheep seemed to become curlier still. He pursued this interesting bit of knowledge, and learned from a sister's biology book that whereas straight hair is round (cylindrical), a cross-section of curly hair shows it to be an ellipse, an oval. The Bavarian boy was intrigued by that knowledge. *Why* was there a difference? Of what importance was it?

One thing led to another and young Karl got away from sheep herding. He served as an apprentice cobbler for his dad but was no good at it. The father, aware of his son's interest in hair, got him a job with the town barber. In that era a barber not only cut hair, he "bled" you if you were sick; he pulled your teeth when they ached; he bandaged your injured hand, arm, leg; he even prescribed some internal medicines. Doctors and dentists were far and few between and not very learned when you did find one. So the barber served, and he held high social and economic status.

Young Karl had little interest in barbering. He felt it was a dull, degrading life. So one day he chucked everything and ran away from home. With his total possessions strapped on him—he was one of the early back packers—he climbed the majestic Alpine slopes into Switzerland and started looking for a job.

In that part of Switzerland German was spoken, so Karl had no language problem. He walked into the first place he saw that seemed to have boys his age employed. It was the small factory of a watchmaker.

"Yes sir, I know about watches." He stretched the truth a bit. "I mean, I can learn fast, sir. I would not want much pay. Just a chance to learn."

That did it. That nearly always does it, when someone applies for work. Karl was put on as a trainee, and stayed there some months. He might have become distinguished in watchmaking but the memories of hair somehow remained strong within him. Sheep hair. Human hair. Straight hair. Curly hair.

One day he did not show up at his job. He walked down to the shop of a hairdresser and represented himself as a talented apprentice, anxious to prove his worth. He was bluffing—but earnest. The bluff worked. He knew about the Marcel Wave, then so popular. Reading had told him it was made with a heated iron, and he had at least seen it applied. So with a bit of common sense and shrewd observation, he managed to keep his new hairdressing job, and even got a small raise in wages.

Fired anew by ambition, handsome young Karl began experimenting with hairdressing techniques of his own.

He had a new theory about making straight hair "permanently" curly. He sweet-talked a young lady who worked with him, Yvonne, into being his first guinea pig.

She thought the idea—and Karl—were wonderful. So she let him pour a mess of glop on her hair and heat it with his irons.

Then the irons were removed.

Yvonne shrieked to high heaven and she left him and her job and even her village. *All* of her lovely hair had been burned off, except for one thick strand.

But that strand made history. It was *permanently* curled. What happened to Yvonne? We don't really know. However, there was a second young lady, Katherina.

Karl married her and they moved to England. They set up a beauty salon in London, and Karl changed his name from Karl Ludwig Nessler to Charles Nestle.

By the year 1905 he and Katherina were doing a good business dressing hair, and especially giving permanents. Karl's chemical-and-heat treatment, toned down after the experience with Yvonne, worked perfectly after he developed the right lotions and application of heat. He became a hair research expert—a far cry from sheep herding or watchmaking. He got written up in big London dailies. In 1906, he rented a big hall in London, invited all the high society ladies, and with considerable fanfare staged a demonstration of permanent hair waving.

Then, millions of women still curled their hair with forked irons heated on top of a kerosene lamp. You would take the irons off the hot glass chimney with a pot holder, spit on the prongs and if they spit back at you,

you were ready to curl your hair. But *that* curling would not last much beyond one evening's party.

Charles Nestle devised a combination of treatments so that the curls stayed in the hair until it grew out straight again, a matter not of hours but of months.

At first, it didn't go over too well—anointing the hair, heating it while one sat six hours in an uncomfortable chair just to make curls that would not straighten out when washed—not too many were willing. Charles was using an alkaline paste, a length of gas pipe, an asbestos tube and charging too much for the process.

But one day in 1914 he had an idea. He posted a sign outside his beauty salon that in brilliant gold letters said "UNDER ROYAL PATRONAGE."

That turned the tide. If any queen, princess, king or prince approved *any*thing—it was made! He had pulled off a major coup.

Many refinements have been made and are continuing. The name of Charles Nestle, the romantic young Bavarian, is not often attached to the methods he invented. But those who benefit from them owe Charles Nestle a vote of thanks for the trade name Permanent Wave.

Chapter 9

"Hey, I'll Break Your Kodak!"

A typical Big Moment has arrived: Thanksgiving or Christmas or graduation from school. No matter; the family is gathering; happy times are in the air, with hearty greetings and laughter for everyone. The home is overflowing; the yard is alive with smiling faces and joyous sounds.

Suddenly, you have an irresistible urge to record the pleasure, the people, the occasion, the scene. You charge off happily shouting "Everybody stay right here!" You come rushing back, shouting orders to your loved ones, who laughingly gather as you direct them, self-consciously shift around, and finally pose for you while you lift a little gadget in your hands.

That is when your cousin is certain to grin wide and say, "HEY, I'LL BREAK YOUR KODAK!"

It is almost sinful NOT to say it; it is part of our habit pattern, our manners and customs. He does not mean that he will resort to physical violence, he is saying that his *image* entering the camera lens will break it.

Kodak. You well know what the word means. Yet it is not what we call a "natural" word, Kodak. It does *not* suggest its appearance or usage; as, for instance, the word "automobile," "bicycle," "typewriter," or "refrigerator" does. It is a proper noun, in such usage as to be virtually a common one. Very few proper nouns ever appear in the dictionary, but kodak does, spelled incorrectly without its capital K. Proper or common, *Kodak* ranks among the most famous names in the world—esteemed, admired, used, cherished, and purchased by the millions.

Kodak is near the top of the great trade names along with Coca Cola. There is a major difference in the two names' origins. One man devised the name "Coca Cola" rather casually and did not expect much to come of it, never dreaming that it would achieve anything akin to national renown. But George Eastman was different.

The Name Was "Doodled" Out.

Young George sat down with paper and pencil, then patiently, deliberately "doodled" out the letters that he hoped would virtually become a synonym for the word *camera.* He was publicity minded, so he wanted something distinctive, some short, unique combination of syllables and sounds that would catch on. It must be easy to spell, pronounce, and remember. He worked at intervals for days, scribbling letters together in helter-skelter form. PIKTUR . . . . PIKTER . . . . PIKTONE . . . . PICK-POK . . . . PICKBOX—hey, *that* one, maybe? PICBOX. It suggested what he wanted it to—pictures made in a box.

Then he mouthed it. Somehow it sounded unpleasant;

too much lip sounds. Also it was too descriptive, too awkward, too contrived.

Thus it went, for a week or more. But George kept at it. Eventually he began to coin words starting with a K sound, as in *c*amera. He kept doodling whenever he had an odd moment, pronouncing the K sounds, seeking a catchy combination.

The Matchless George Eastman.

George's home was in Rochester, New York. His family was very poor. His mother was widowed, and he had two sisters, one of whom was crippled. Young George had to scrounge around getting whatever jobs he could find to earn a few dollars. Things took a turn for the better when he turned age 15; an insurance company hired him for $3 a week, a good sum for the time. George had to sweep the insurance office floors every night and wash out the cuspidors.

George worked hard, was self-reliant and dependable; therefore, he soon got a better job at $5 a week. He began studying accounting at night. When he turned his 20th birthday he got a job in a bank, earning $800 a year. This was the moment when young George began to dream seriously about owning a camera some day.

He began to read everything he could find about photography. Not much was printed on the subject. Much of his scientific information came from a magazine published in England. But he did learn that those early plates of tin and glass had to be exposed when the chemicals on them were still *wet*, and realized what a nuisance that must be. One thing led to another, and soon George

was buying chemicals and pans and experimenting in his
mother's kitchen at home.

At first it was purely a hobby; work at the bank all
day, putter around with chemicals at night. Sometimes
friends would drop in, lured by the magic of photography.

The Dry Plate.

George went on with his kitchen chemistry, and one day
he said to a friend, "I must find a way to make a photographic plate that can be exposed when it is *dry*!"

He was staying up so late at night that he would doze
at his desk next day. Even when he forced himself to stay
alert, his mind would drift off, exploring possibilities that
had nothing to do with banking but much to do with
photography. He almost got fired at the bank. There
were occasions when he even slept the night—or what remained of the night after long hours of experimenting—rolled in a blanket on the kitchen floor. Other
inventors, explorers, and innovators have been similarly
obsessed, or perhaps the better word is dedicated.

Finally, George Eastman perfected his dry plate for
making photographic negatives.

But the device was expensive and cumbersome. Cam-
eras of that day all had massive stands, bellows, knobs,
ratchets, wheels, lenses, tripods, and endless inconven-
iences. Often two men were required just to lift a professional camera onto a wagon. And holders for the new dry
plates took up outrageous room in storage, because of the
required insulation against breakage. This impelled
George Eastman to put his mind to work again. He kept
demanding, "Why do the plates have to be glass? Why

does the camera have to be so big and bulky? Why can't we scale everything down?"

Film on Rolls.

George saved a modest amount of money, and in 1880 leased the third floor of an old building in Rochester and converted that into a laboratory for his research. He also made and sold sensitized dry plates of glass, meanwhile working to reduce the size of everything. Of course plastics were unknown at that time. But a similar material did appear, a celluloid. George began experimenting with that.

He produced dry "negative" film pictures, in sequence, on rolls instead of plates, so that the film would move through the back of the camera when the operator turned a knob. The film was not fragile like glass. It was much lighter in weight and much cheaper to produce. It was first marketed in 1889.

Even so, the total number of photographers was limited—only a few hundred professionals were in existence, and virtually no amateurs at all. George needed people to buy his film. He had made a fundamental mistake: he had created a product before there was much of a market for it. So he set out to create the market.

His answer to the problem was to design a small, hand-held camera which the public at large could buy at reasonable cost and use with reasonable ease. Again he was successful, and his small hand camera became yet another advance in photography.

George's camera was not small by today's standard. It was a squarish box in which you might have packed four baseballs. It weighed 22 ounces. The lens in it was fast enough for taking instantaneous pictures; people no longer had to freeze motionless for one to ten seconds to have portraits made. The pictures it took were round, 2½ inches in diameter. It had a fixed or "universal" focus in its lens; nobody had to worry about distances. You just stepped out into the sunlight and began snapping pictures. In fact it was necessary only to obey the advertising published by the new Eastman Kodak Company—"You press the button, we do the rest."

The slogan intrigued people. They made a new thing of it. For instance, if brother and sister were assigned to do the supper dishes, sister might poke her finger hard onto brother's front shirt button and say, "I pressed the button, *you* do the rest!" then drop her dish towel and run. The baseball coach at school would smile and cleverly tell his team, "I only press the button, you do the rest." The command, "Hey, press the button!" came to mean stop lazing around, get going, move it, get to work—slang of the day. It found hundreds of expressions, and George Eastman was delighted; it was publicizing his new camera and costing him nothing.

With your new, inexpensive, small camera—which was often mispronounced ca-MEER-a in that period—you would snap almost literally everything in sight, then mail the entire camera with the exposed roll of film to the Eastman Kodak laboratories in Rochester. They would develop and print your pictures then return them with your camera reloaded. "What won't they think of next?" people kept asking in amazement. Meanwhile, everyone dithered, wondering if their pictures would come out. One big difference was there were 100 exposures on a roll back then, whereas today the number usually is 20 or 36. Also, while today's negatives are much smaller, today's prints are larger than those 2½-inch circles, with a choice of dimensions.

Kodak.

The explosive success of his early, inexpensive camera prompted George Eastman to sit down and doodle out the name KODAK. He registered it on September 4, 1888, in the United States Patent Office in Washington. (He also tried to register the word CAMERA at the same time, but the Patent Office ruled that the word was not subject to exclusive usage and was in fact a common noun for everyone to use.)

Right away "Kodak" took, much as Eastman's press-the-button slogan had. People stopped saying camera and began saying Kodak. Later people did the same with "Victrola," and for a while with "Frigidaire." It worried George. He had his advertising agency blast the nation with the statement that "Only Eastman makes KODAK." He did not want some opportunist with another picturebox to poach on his territory.

Very soon, too, Mr. Eastman got away from the nuisance of having everybody send the camera to Rochester. He made it possible for people to remove the exposed film and send it without the camera, but the company continued to send new film back along with the prints. He wanted to milk as much profit as possible from the sale of film, and this forced continuity did pay off for a while. Then the inconvenience became too great a problem, and so the unexposed films were made available at the "corner drug" or similar store, much as they are today.

Rapid Advances.

The original sensitized roll of film had a paper base, which was soon changed to transparent cellulose. One problem at that stage was the film had to be loaded into the Kodak in a darkroom. No one had a darkroom at home. Even if you contrived one in a dark closet or attic at night, you still had to load the film into the Kodak by *feel* only—an awkward process. Some help came when it was learned that red light would not harm or expose the film, but providing red light at home was also a nuisance. The problem was solved by backing the sensitized film with a strip of nonactinic paper, so that the Kodak could be reloaded easily in daylight. This technique is still used, and developing it added more millions to the Eastman profits.

Mr. Eastman's expanding business brought many talented scientists to his laboratories in Rochester. Soon after the first universal focus camera appeared, they developed one with variable focus which made all the photos much sharper in detail. More and more refinements were added to the popular box camera.

The first folding camera appeared in 1891. The first pocket-sized Kodak came in 1895, but it reverted to the box type, and made negatives 1½-by-2 inches. The first folding-pocket Kodak was offered to the public in 1898. Despite all those advances, millions of Americans clung to the original box type, and nobody was quite sure why. You can still find it in use today, although few are now on the retail market. New compact designs have come along, with everything in a small package.

Soon everybody had some kind of Kodak, or so it seemed; at least one per family seemed almost a necessity. Almost every child age 10 or over asked for a Kodak at Christmas or for a birthday gift. Happily, the price went down and down in those days before World War I. Eastman made most of its profit through sale of film and prints.

By 1915 thousands of people were printing their own pictures. Equipment was simple and inexpensive. You started with a small printing frame that held the negative flat against sensitized paper. You would expose this to a white electric light for a few seconds, learning by experiment. Then under red light you would immerse the exposed piece of paper in a special chemical solution in a soup bowl or the like.

Slowly the photo image would come out, that is, take form in detail, as you gently shook the piece of paper in the developing solution. When you thought it was just right in proper black-and-white tones, you quickly moved the photo into a rinse, thence into a fixing bath in another soup bowl. The second chemical stopped the image-growing process and fixed it permanently. After a few minutes, you carefully placed the wet photo on a sheet of glass or metal, and left it to dry. The next day you could take of packet of homemade pictures to school.

"Kodak" therefore became the name, world-renowned, for what still is possibly the greatest toy ever invented. It was more than a plaything—it encouraged creative art, it stimulated the imagination, it gave you something memorable, it recorded facets of human life.

George Eastman, the boy who once had gladly swept floors and polished spittoons for $3 a week, is honored among immortal Americans of industry and art. But strangely enough very few photographs ever were taken of this man who made photography popular. He was known as a pleasant person and became a generous philanthropist who gave more than $100 million to help upgrade American education before his death in 1932.

Chapter 10

"Guaranteed to Shrink and Fade and Last Forever"

Four teenagers paused before the window of a clothing store. Behind the glass was a display of trousers. They were all of an indigo blue color and in various sizes. But a sign near them in big letters was startling. It said:

THESE LEVI'S ARE GUARANTEED TO SHRINK AND FADE AND LAST FOREVER

The haberdasher knew his customers. He knew that young folk wanted the "in" thing.

And the "in" thing in pants for many years has been, and still is, Levi jeans, jeans guaranteed to shrink and fade and last forever—"forever" meaning for the life of the pants. Levi's rank as the Number One pants in North America, South America, much of Europe and Asia. It is the most valuable trade name in the garment industry. This does not discredit competitors. It merely points up the factor of circumstance, the escalating quality of fame that can sometime be started by seemingly trivial incidents and events. Let's take a look at the Levi story.

The Tent Maker.

You will recall that in 1848 a prospector named John Marshall was poking around in an isolated California stream near a point called Sutter's Mill, when he casually picked up a rock that glittered. True, all that glitters is not gold, but the glitter in Marshall's rock was genuine. History was about to be made.

When the news got around, the greatest gold rush in history was triggered. Eager people began streaming to California over land, while others rode great sailships around the Horn, up the long coast of South America and on into beautiful San Francisco Bay.

Among those sailing was a handsome twenty-year-old immigrant from Bavaria, whose parents had been tailors and clothiers. His name was Levi Strauss.

Levi quickly decided *not* to rush into the hills with pick, shovel and metal basin for panning. He knew nothing about such techniques and he was not an outdoorsman. Moreover, he guessed that the gold fields would already be overcrowded when he arrived. But he knew the miners would need fabrics. So he packed big trunks with bolts of broadcloth, a few linens, silks, and especially a big supply of canvas.

He predicted that the canvas would be much in demand for tents, to be used by hardy souls out in the hills. He could import more canvas, and felt that as a tent-maker he could net a fortune.

Panting for Pants.

"We don't need no tents," an old grizzled prospector rumbled at Levi, when he had landed and offered his canvas for sale. "We can build us a lean-to shack that'll do better, or cut ourselves into a cave that will protect us from storms better'n cloth will. Son, if you got any good sense, make that canvas into pants."

Levi looked at him in surprise. "Pants?"

"That's right. More'n anything, we need good, strong pants out there. They ain't none to be had, none worth havin'. Nothin' but weak stuff. We're always havin' to stop our mining to get another set. Could you make me a good pair of pants with some of that canvas? I'd pay you a hundred dollars."

The words of that conversation are imaginary, but not at all far-fetched. The talk did take place, and Levi himself told of it many times in years to come.

A hundred dollars for one pair of rough canvas pants, worth maybe two dollars back home in New York City?

"I will have them ready for you by sundown tonight," Levi promised.

The old miner was delighted with them pants. What was a hundred dollars? He had picked up more than that in half an hour of gold panning. The new canvas pair "set him up grand" in his own estimation and in that of his colleagues. He showed them off proudly.

"These pants," he told them, "are *Levi's*."

He used that word as a possessive, meaning they had been made by a fellow named Levi.

But the listeners made the word a straight noun, thereby launching a trade name. Not mere pants but

Levi's, a synonym implying high quality. They looked good and were strong too. "Where is this fellow?" they asked. "Can we get him to make us some?"

Young Levi Strauss worked his fingers to the bone sewing up canvas Levi's to order. It was a shame he had no such gadget as a sewing machine; but its time had not come. He plied needle and thread zealously until his eyes burned with fatigue—two or three pairs a day, two or three hundred dollars. Levi was getting rich quick from the California gold fields, even if he wasn't digging in them.

The fame of the trade name *Levi's* spread rapidly and its owner made the most of it. Young Strauss barely had time to eat and sleep.

Levi's canvas did not prove to be as strong as he and his customers hoped it might; it did not stand the strain of mining. Levi therefore ordered a newer and stronger kind of cloth with which to make his pants: denim. By the early 1870s he had discontinued canvas altogether and was importing big quantities of denim. In the world of tailoring denim had never before amounted to much, but it was heavily used for making sails. Levi reasoned that it might be just the ticket for the needs of miners. Events proved him to be correct.

Blue Denim.

He specified that all his ordered denim be dyed a rather dull indigo blue. Bright blue would be too showy, and prone to reveal smudges and dirt. The indigo shade blended in with the shadows of rocks, hills and trees, thus was good camouflage from enemies. And the color pleased the customers. Blue denim made much better-looking and better-wearing trousers than had the tent canvas.

There in the gold-boom regions of California, every man soon wanted Levi's. Mr. Strauss advertised for helpers, and did manage to get a few seamstresses, but they were quickly married away from him. Then a few men tailors came from back East, and in time he had a competent crew to help him.

Riveted!

An old bearded prospector called Alkali Ike came into town one day with his Levi's pockets ragged and torn from carrying tools and rock specimens. Alkali got drunk and roared over to one of Levi's tailors Jacob W. Davis and complained about his pockets.

Finally Mr. Davis wearied of the old man, put him to bed to sleep it off, and removed his dirty denim pants. Mr. Davis brought the pants up the street to the local harness shop to rivet the bottom corners of the pocket to strengthen them. He returned and slipped the Levi's back onto the sleeping prospector.

Weeks later, Alkali Ike came back to town, went to Davis the tailor and praised him highly. Those pockets had carried the heaviest iron and ore samples, and the rivets had held.

Levi Strauss immediately had the idea of copper-riveting his pants patented.

Since then many millions of Levi's have been produced with rivets, not necessarily from need, but as a touch of distinction, a hint of ornamentation. Decades later, rivets are still in most of the Levi's produced.

Let Them Shrink!

Somewhere along the decades, another development in Levi's occurred. The original supplies of blue denim from eastern textile mills came to Levi Strauss without being preshrunk. Very probably this was to save the cost of shrinking. Therefore Levi had to make his pants a bit larger than the customer needed, with the understanding that they would indeed shrink to proper size when the first rain fell on them.

Meanwhile, almost every other fabric being sold in piece goods form, or even in tailored clothing, was shrunk before being sold. Why didn't Levi Strauss and Company come to that?

Because the customers didn't *want* their blue denim jeans preshrunk. The ritual of letting Levi's shrink to near skin tightness became the fad, and still is.

Changes are inevitable. In recent years, some Levi's have been marketed without the copper pocket rivets. Some have appeared in red denim, and embroidered.

By 1978 approximately one *billion* pairs of Levi's were sold. They are the only item of North American wearing apparel whose style has remained basically the same for more than 125 years.

Levi Straus's original one-man tailor shop grew over the years to an industry with about 30,000 employees. This makes it not only America's largest apparel maker, but one of the largest corporations anywhere. It operates almost 80 plants in North America, Asia and western Europe.

In all fairness, one thought must be repeated: Levi's are not the only good-quality blue denim pants. Strauss competitors also have excellent garments. Even so, Levi's is economically at the top of the heap.

A small light blue tab is still sewn onto the side of one hip pocket. It carries one sewn-in word—*LEVI'S.*

Notice the apostrophe, used to indicate a possessive. It says in effect that these pants belong to Levi Strauss. They don't, but the possessive is an enduring tribute to the man who originated them. It is the company's official trademark, but relatively few people realize that. In fact the apostrophe is generally lost or ignored, so that LEVIS—without the apostrophe—is the form in common usage.

Also there is an identifying soft-leather label sewn into the belt line of many pants models, especially those worn by cowboys. This, too, is an officially registered trademark. It has some nice words, but the focal point is the world-famous picture, looking as though it were burned into the leather, showing two early-day westerners with whips making two horses pull hard in opposite directions. Tied to their harness traces is a pair of Levi's. The horses are straining to tear the pants apart—with no success.

Those identifying trade-name insignia are regarded as symbols of discrimination in attire. They lend status.

The advertising says, "guaranteed to last forever." Well, a few years ago workers constructing a new shopping center in Sacramento, California, near the original gold fields, had to move an old cemetery. One grave, dated 1871, contained the remains of an old-timer in a pair of Levi's. Although his coffin had disintegrated, *the Levi pants were still in fair condition.*

Chapter 11
Z-Z-Z-Z-Z-Z-Zip!

Who in the world ever dreamed up such a weird contrivance as the zipper?

It is one of our small but taken-for-granted blessings. We do not know how it works, we simply work it. We snatch on a skirt or dress, we leap into trousers, zip up the metal talon tab, and off we go.

Until recently, we had to laboriously fasten buttons into little holes, holes which tended to be too tight or too large. That was a way of life. Now we can zip up quickly, dependably, and neatly. Zippers have revolutionized the business of fastening or unfastening fabric to fabric.

The astounding zipper was conceived in the nineteenth century—a fact that surprises almost everybody, because we assume it is a modern marvel. But conceiving is one thing, production and selling are others. The zipper did not burgeon overnight.

Credit for the actual invention of the zipper probably should go to Whitcomb Judson. Records to the U.S. Patent Office show that in 1893 he was awarded sole legal ownership of a device named a "Clasp Locker or Unlocker for Shoes."

Shoes had long been made of either wood or animal skins, mostly the latter. Probably sandals were the very first items devised to protect the feet, and most likely they were tied on with strings of animal rawhide. Shoes through the ages were tied on, or buttoned or laced up.

Mr. Judson's new device was innovative and created quite a stir. At first it did not occur to anyone that it might also be adapted to trousers, shirts, coats, blouses, and skirts as well as shoes. Later, he did campaign for its use on corsets. These had always been laced with stout cords. Now there was a metal mechanical gadget for them.

Unfortunately it did not work. In fact the locker-or-unlocker did not work very well even on shoes. Tested on gloves and leggings, it still wasn't dependable. Once closed, it tended to pop open or gap. Whit Judson lost his enthusiasm for the device.

But a fellow named Lewis Walker came along and became intrigued with what people were calling Judson's "Slide Fastener." He revived Judson's enthusiasm for the invention. After two years of long and costly experiments, the two men offered the world their new "Universal Fastener." This was a chain of curved, flat hooks that could be attached to a parallel chain of open links by moving a little metal slider along the union line. The Universal Fastener, it was said, would revolutionize the closing of shoes. Corsets, gloves and leggings seemed momentarily forgotten. A patent was granted in 1902.

Again, there was no success. The invention was still too crude, too full of bugs. The costly machine constructed to manufacture it did not function well. People could not afford to pay the price deemed necessary for a Universal Fastener. So, Judson and Walker kept on working.

C-Curity.

This time Walker and Judson evolved a fabric strip to which they sewed metal links instead of using a metal chain. This was in 1904, when a newly formed Hook and Eye Company was opened in Hoboken, New Jersey, to manufacture the remodeled device. Tiny metal bits on one side of the slider were called hooks, those on the other side were called eyes. The slider would unite or open them; all the user had to do was exert a slight pull and shoes, pants, or gloves could be made secure.

The key word was *secure* because it became the root of the first great trade name in this field. Judson and Walker brainstormed it, and came up with the name C-CURITY PLACKET FASTENER. It told much. A "placket" is an opening in a skirt, dress, or blouse, and if it could be snugly fastened it would look better than a row of buttons.

Published advertisements followed with variations which said, "Your Skirt is Always Securely Fastened with a C-Curity. A Gentle Pull Does It."

Once more, that "always" was misleading, because the weird little device still tended to pop open under stress. It failed completely on corsets.

The two partners hired a Swedish genius named Gideon Sundback to restudy the C-Curity and make it perfect. He altered the original hook-and-eye, and a patent was obtained under the new name, "Plako."

Too few people seemed interested. The firm faced

financial trouble as well as technical trouble. But Gideon
Sundbeck kept on tinkering, experimenting, straining for
perfection. He abandoned the hook-and-eye concept and
came up with two new ideas which were patented. Mr.
Walker again supplied necessary money, and in 1913 a
new Hookless Fastener Company was announced. During the next few years almost 80 patents were granted to
Mr. Sundbeck in his efforts to improve the fastener. By
the year 1914 he and Mr. Walker had "Hookless No. 2"
on the market, but it was 1917 before any big manufacturer would even consider it. When one did agree to give
it a try, it was the U.S. Navy, which purchased 35,000 of
the new fasteners for use on sailors' money belts and
flying suits. Next it was used on purses and tobacco
pouches. Then, in 1923, Goodrich Rubber Company
tried them on heavy overshoes called galoshes. That test
trial gave us the device we use today. A Goodrich executive tried the fastener, liked it, and exclaimed to his colleagues, "Go ahead, zip 'er up!"

They zipped, and liked the quickness, the new sure-
hold quality which had come at last, so they ordered
150,000 of the now perfected hookless fasteners.

Talon "Claws".

To do the zipping, a little metal tab had to be held in
your fingers. Somebody said this looked like a bird of
prey grasping at something with its claws, or talons.
Wherefore the name "TALON ZIPPER."

Today zippers are used to close and open just about
everything from shirt fronts to trousers to bed rolls to
pockets to purses to shoes to tents to suitcases, and so on.

In fact the Talon Company in 1978 was manufacturing more than 1,000 *miles* of zipper tape every *day*, and the demand was still growing.

As with many other trade-name products, "zip" and "zipper" entered the folk language. "Zip your lip" was already an expression often heard. "Zip along" meant to go faster, speed up.

But still they aren't foolproof. In 1977, a balloonist in California got carried ten miles beyond his planned destination. Asked why, he replied, "My zipper got stuck, so that I couldn't open the bag of lifting gas."

Chapter 12

Fun and Games

One weekend in 1977 more than 10,000 people gathered in a park at Houston, Texas, to have competitive fun throwing, or watching other people throw, a small, cupped "pie pan" around. Later that year another multitude gathered in the Rose Bowl at Pasadena, California, to pursue the same sport.

Meanwhile at every ocean beach, lake resort, playground and park in the United States, millions more were paired off, standing twenty to one hundred yards apart, sailing the same type of "pan" back and forth. Sometimes groups formed triangles, squares or circles, keeping two or three of the devices going at once.

No over-exertion, no expensive equipment, no danger, just wholesome recreation, and superb exercise and fellowship at negligible cost.

Perhaps you have engaged in this new and seemingly enduring American sport: tossing a "flying saucer" made of plastic—most editions of which are marketed under the copyrighted trade name, *Frisbee.*

By 1970 Frisbee flingers seemed to be everywhere. By 1978 their numbers had more than doubled. By 1990, statisticians project there will be at least one Frisbee for every living soul on the North American continent. Competitive items of similar design were having a good run, too, but nowhere near the sales of the original.

Consider
the Ball.

The flat "pie pan" disc cupped for aerodynamic or aerobatic quality has almost replaced the ball.

Almost any ball can cause damage—break window glass, conk you on the head and knock you into the hospital, even slay you on occasion. Thousands of people have been badly injured or even killed by baseballs.

But a Frisbee is nearly harmless. It is light in weight. It sails at relatively slow speed compared to a thrown ball. If it does hit someone, the person will only be startled, not really hurt. In fact he or she probably will retrieve it, smiling, and flip it back to you. The exercise is not too strenuous and is genuine fun.

You can throw it in a multitude of curves much more artistic than the flight of any spherical ball. If it veers into the water or lake or sea, the next wave will bring it to shore for you, because it floats. If it sails over the backyard fence and whams into your neighbor's window, nothing will happen; the glass won't break because the Frisbee is "soft" compared to a bulletlike ball. It won't even do much damage if it gets windborne and is carried into a bed of delicate flowers.

Frisbee Just
"Happened".

The Frisbee producers are not too well-known. There is
no Henry Ford among them; no introverted genius
Thomas Edison; no Wright Brothers. But there is a nice
guy named Walter F. Morrison, who maybe ought to
have a statue erected in his honor somewhere. He "discovered" and developed the flying platter.

In 1949, Walter visited a New England college campus
and saw some students tossing pie pans discarded from a
bakery. He was intrigued by those tins being tossed back
and forth.

Walter Morrison was already well into the manufacturing and sale of another unique toy—the Hula Hoop.
Now he went back to his Hula Hoop factory and quickly
developed a mock-up pie tin of polyethylene. He made
several types, testing them, and had the best ones patented. He called the new little toy a "Plutoplatter" after the
distant planet soaring through the skies. As a trade name,
Plutoplatter was not bad, was in fact catchy.

By 1970 Walt Morrison was a millionaire because
many people had bought Plutoplatters and were sailing
them arund. At that time, his huge factory in San Ga-
briel, California, was selling them at the rate of 100,000
per day. That came to 35,500,000 Plutoplatters a year. In
1973, for some unaccountable reason, another spurt in
sales began. No big special advertising or publicity campaign had been launched. It just seemed that everybody
suddenly began wanting a pie-plate plastic toy to throw
around.

The trade name "Plutoplatter" soon went through a

sort of metamorphosis. It was dubbed Flying Saucer, Salad Plate, Bucket Top, Skipper, Floater, Tosser, and so forth. Then one day Mr. Morrison was watching high school boys throw it hard. It hit a cement slab and seemed to leap off with extra force.

"Wham-O!"

One of the boys called out loudly, "WHAM-O, there she goes!"

The firm that sells the toy is now known as the Wham-O Manufacturing Company. And for a while the official name of the toy itself was Wham-O.

But time changes things. More listening was done, more thinking. "Wham-O" lacked something as a selling name. It suggested collision, hitting, even destructive force. What would be a better name?

Its owners gave serious study to the matter, and soon were harking back to the platter's origin, when Walter Morrison saw boys throwing empty pie pans discarded from a bakery. Research showed it to be the Frisbee Bakery in New England. Frisbee is a pleasant sound, easy to read, pronounce, and remember.

Walter Morrison, head man of the Wham-O Manufacturing Company, said that "Frisbee is a ridiculous trade name for anything" because it is meaningless. But you can't argue with success. It is no more ridiculous than is "Wham-O" as the name for a multi-million-dollar corporation.

What's in a name anyway?

Well, at this writing, there are at least 100 million Frisbees flipping through the air around the world, so perhaps the answer to that question is—100 million dollars.

Chapter 13

"Get Out and Get Under..."

In all our national history, what person has most changed the American way of life?

It is an intriguing question. You will think immediately of George Washington, Thomas Jefferson, Abraham Lincoln, or of Einstein.

How about Henry Ford, whose name became the most important trade name of all time?

In his lifetime he made over not only our nation but much of the world. It is unbelievable until you consider carefully what he achieved. But for what he did, your own life today would be vastly different.

To understand why, we must first envision one aspect of America from its beginning until about 1920.

In that long stretch, the pacing of life was relatively slow, relaxed, and easygoing. For one thing, we generally stayed put. We did not travel around the continent much. Roads were few and poor—there were a few explorers, surveyors, frontiersmen, pioneers and military men. But generally the members of any family stayed put.

Civil War Baby.

In the year 1863, when America was at its lowest ebb, a baby boy was born to an obscure farm family, the Fords, and named Henry. The growing Henry worked hard as a small boy helping his family, but he did not like farming.

His bent was more toward repairing, maintaining and even producing the few mechanical tools and machines the farms had in that postwar era. He liked to poke into machine shops where engines and wheels were being made or repaired. The railroad train had come along. That smoke-belching monster with its loud bell and whistle shriek was a marvel to Henry and he studied it with awe. Other engines, powered crudely by steam, also were in use now to pump water, saw wood, and such.

So Henry got himself a job in a machine shop.

Then he became enchanted with another marvel—electricity. The use of electricity was a new force on the world scene in post-Civil-War years, as innovative minds experimented with it.

"Wouldn't it be great," Henry said to his friends, "if we could make a buggy that would run on its own power like a train locomotive, and not have to have horses pulling it?"

But then it seemed impossible.

However, pretty soon somebody *did* invent a motorized buggy. Today there is argument as to just who the inventor was. It wasn't Henry. Several men, working independently, contributed to it.

But Henry Ford was to make it practical.

Henry was only sixteen when he became a machinist's apprentice. But then Thomas Edison had come on the scene and Henry moved to a better job, becoming chief engineer of the new Edison Illuminating Company in Detroit.

In the Beginning.

He actually began his experimenting with motorized buggies in 1890. Three years later he came out with the first Ford automobile. It was a low-slung, little buggy with four, large, spider-web wheels of equal size on standard buggy axles. But under its seat was a "one-lunger" engine. He had made the lone cylinder from a short length of exhaust pipe off a steam engine. A flywheel was made not of metal but wood. A chain belt connected with the buggy wheels.

The driver sat in the single seat and held a lever or tiller much like that on a boat. If any obstruction appeared in the roadway ahead, you tinkled a little bell on the front of the dashboard. There was no "hood" as we know it; none was needed. There was no top, hence no windows or curtains; no trunk, no running boards or fenders. But it ran at 20 miles an hour, and that was marvel enough.

People by the thousands came to see beaming Henry Ford in his brown suit and derby hat go rolling along. Horses and mules would rear up, snort, paw the earth, and bolt when Henry chug-chugged within smelling and listening range. Some people called the contraption an instrument of the devil.

The cars during those formative years often belched, stopped and conked out dead—smelling and sizzling and smoking a bit. The driver would have to remove his cap

and goggles and the beige linen duster-robe that he wore
to protect his clothing, sigh prodigiously, then set to work
with hand tools, hoping he could cope.

"You Gotta Get Under."

That situation became famous on the American scene. It
gave the nonmotorists a happy comeback. They would
see a stricken motorist and shout "Get a horse!" Also, the
stalled motorist begat a popular song which swept the
nation:

> You gotta get under,
> Get out and get under—

which was often true!

Magazine and newspaper cartoonists pictured many
such episodes. Many songs spread across the nation. One
said quite frankly, "If I can afford a Ford, you can afford
to marry me." A competitor's song had more musical
beauty. Its title was *In My Merrie Oldsmobile*. Parodies on
all horseless-carriage songs were heard everywhere; jokes
about the vehicles were rampant. In short, the social impact of the new cars was profound. And most of the talk,
the jokes and wisecracks, the cute-but-silly songs, were di-
rected at Henry's popular open-air buggy without a
horse in front.

Henry Ford did not spring instantly to success and
fame. He did a long, tedious stretch of experimenting,
testing, straining, revising, and hoping. And you should
see the first horseless carriage that he made.

And you can. The odd-looking contraption is in a mu-
seum in Dearborn, Michigan, and it still runs.

He began manufacturing his new car in a factory at Highland Park, Michigan, and sold it at a price the "ordinary" householder could pay. No longer was the automobile a "plaything of the rich."

Ford reached maximum stride about the year 1908, with a vastly upgraded car called the Model T.

Before 1927 he had sold 15 million copies of it!

It had become "the poor man's horseless carriage." Almost any man with a good job could afford the few hundred dollars that the Model T cost. Moreover, millions of owners soon felt confidence in being their own auto mechanics. Manuals that came with the Model T taught you how to repair it when needed. It was said that anyone with a pair of pliers, a screwdriver and a length of hay-baling wire, could keep his Model T in good running order just by tinkering with it in the home backyard. Contrast that with the highly complicated and costly "service jobs" that owners are forced to face today.

Many competitors got into the car business, and their grand names also enrich our business history and our folklore. But because the unimposing Ford was *the* car for so long, it stood out as a trade name.

At one time more than half the "horseless carriages" in America came from the factory that Henry Ford launched.

The coming of the automobile completely changed America. We were no longer homebound with limited horizons. By the year 1950, our nation had become so fluid, so prone to shift about, go places, get new jobs and see new climes, that the average time they lasted in one home was five years. Mostly due to that farm lad turned machinist, the boy named Henry.

And, perhaps even more important, Henry Ford revolutionized the manufacturing world, the factory system, with his production-line techniques turning out more cars, more cheaply.

**A New Idea in
Manufacturing.**

Mr. Ford got mass production on His Model T by originating the now-famous factory assembly line. In this, each mechanic would have just one specific job to do. Theretofore, each man might have had to work on all parts of a car; now he was a specialist.

Ford also shocked the business world by establishing a minimum wage of $5 a day for his factory workers. The going wage in other factories had long been from $1 to $2.50 a day. This increase caused him to be hailed as a great benefactor.

Because of constant experimenting and improving, the good old Model T eventually gave way to a vastly better Model A. The latter had a self-starter. It had electric instead of acetylene lights, a generally better mechanical system, and a much more appealing set of body designs. Again his car sold into the millions. But by now, as you will know, other astute geniuses had launched stiff competition, hence he did not hog the national car market this time.

In 1932 he did bring out a car with a major change in the motor. Until then most motors had been four-cylinder varieties. Now Henry offered the world eight cylinders, molded in metal to form an angle. This V-8 engine is still in use.

When World War I came along, the then-renowned Henry Ford was against it. An idealist, he felt that European nations were very foolish, and that if someone could just get to their leaders they could be talked into calling off the war.

Who else but Henry Ford himself? So in 1915 he chartered, outfitted and manned a Peace Ship which he sailed to Norway, hoping to attract leaders of the warring nations to that neutral country to sit down with him across a table and reach a truce. He had 150 people on his ship, everything paid for by him. But the idea came to nothing. In fact some people ridiculed and scoffed at him.

When the United States entered the war, Henry Ford quickly retooled his vast factories so that they could make war materiel. He also became an avid philanthropist, endowing museums and hospitals.

The Tin Lizzie.

It is impossible to say too much about those early Fords. They literally permeated and regulated the lives of all the people. They acquired the nickname, Tin Lizzie. Around the turn of this century, "Lizzie" was a nickname for any family's maid-of-all-work, a willing and dependable servant. The Ford was like that.

Such acceptance delighted Henry. It amounted to priceless advertising. He reveled in the knowledge that he, almost singlehandedly, had remade our economic and social lives by vastly broadening our travel range and our levels of production.

INDEX

ABOUT THE AUTHOR

OREN ARNOLD—
is one of America's most prolific freelance writers.

Eighty-five of his books have been published. Others are under contract and on the presses.

Book subjects include family life matters, personal guidance, biographies, travel, adventure, and humor, for both adults and juveniles. Most works have been nonfiction; but one became a first-prize-winning Literary Award Novel.

He has published nearly 2,000 articles in the major magazines. These include many originals for The Reader's Digest, The Saturday Evening Post, Better Homes and Gardens, American Home, Boys Life, Esquire, True, Coronet, Home Life, numerous others. For 20 years he has written a monthly page of commentary in one big journal, and similar pages in five others. He has been called the "most quoted columnist in America," and has received many honors.

Born and reared on a ranch in Texas, Mr. Arnold spent five years in Rice University. He and his wife Adele live in Laguna Beach, California. They travel extensively, world wide. At home, he works about five hours a day at his typewriter. He also lectures and appears often on television and radio. Both he and Mrs. Arnold are very active in their church, and in family-life counseling.

C 1

DATE			
MAY 2 3 1997			
NOV 3 0 1998			

© THE BAKER & TAYLOR CO.